TOUCH THE SKY

RASHMI BANSAL

TOUCH THE SKY

BUSHFIRE PUBLISHERS

First Published by Westland -2019

Reprinted by **Bushfire Publishers LLP- 2022**
(Venture by Rashmi Bansal)
Core House, Off CG Road, Near Parimal Garden
Ahmedabad 380006

Bushfire and the Bushfire logo are the trademarks of Bushfire Publishers LLP, or its affiliates.

ISBN: 978-81-947679-1-6
Design by Haitenlo Semy

Printed at Thomson Press (I) Ltd.

No part of this book may be reproduced, or stored in a retrieval system, or transmitted in any form or by any means, electronic, mechanical, photocopying, recording, or otherwise, without express written permission of the publisher.

This book was researched and written by Bloody Good Book (division of Bushfire Publishers, a venture by Rashmi Bansal)

Dedicated to

My priya chachiji Pratima Garg

you believed I could fly

Contents

Acknowledgements

Thank you to the Zee team for conceiving the idea and putting their faith in me, to bring it to life.

The viewers of Zee TV who responded to our call to crowd-source stories.

The team at Bloody Good Book - Niyati Patel, who was the spine of this project, and the wind beneath my wings.

Suman Chhabria Addepalli, for identifying, interviewing and drafting two of the stories in the book (Shital Bhatkar and Apeksha Shah).

Aliya Bashir for identifying and interviewing Hafiza Khan in Srinagar.

Semy for the evocative cover design and my editor Deepthi for keenly going through the copy.

All the women who honestly and willingly shared their stories with us.

Lata, Nivi and Maya, who each love me in their own way. And make me feel complete.

Author's Note

My grandmother Badam bai was a 'pious lady', married at age 16, bore a child at 18. Never went to school. She raised nine children, observed all festivals, cooked on a *koyle ka chulha*. Her *makke ki roti* and *doodhiya kheech* were to die for. All her life, she wore saris, *wo bhi sar dhak kar*.

Badam bai was a gentle soul but she wielded power, within the home.

My mother Manorama is a home-maker, a double MA, had an arranged marriage. She raised two children, observes some festivals, cooks on LPG, drives a car. Her banana muffins and *tadkewali dal* are out of this world.

She once wore saris but now lives in kurtas and lycra churidars.

My mom is the soft power that keeps our family together.

I am a career woman, an MBA, adventure-seeker, juggling many balls in the air. I have one daughter, rarely observe festivals, use the microwave, travel for my work. I cook when I feel like it, leaving the rest to my housekeeper. I love my jeans and hate wearing dupattas.

I am a modern woman, with the power to impact the world.

In India, we know power as Shakti — it is a feminine dimension. The Energy of Creation.

Each of us has the power to create a life on the foundations of truth, beauty and strong self-belief.

This book is about women who have taken that inner journey. Of finding themselves, and the power that lies within.

You have always been powerful, you just didn't know it, you just didn't show it.

Take charge of your life, exercise your power. You are not a victim of circumstance, of society, of any external force.

Apne andar ki shakti ko jaaniye, pehchaaniye. Aaj se likhiye apna ek sunehra kal. Be that passionate, positive, powerful person you were born to be.

Ziddi

"Beti, zid mat kar" – ma-baap kehte hain.
Lekin duniya ka har bada kaam, acchha kaam,
naya kaam, zid se hi hua hai!*

*Do not be stubborn (ziddi), parents tell their daughters.
But every new idea, big idea, good idea has come into being
because of unshakeable belief.

Having a Ball

Yuwa Girls
Hutup village, Jharkhand

"Bachchi hai toh kya – she has to do the housework." Rinky, Kusum, Kiran and Mansi always did what they were told. But they did one small thing without asking for permission. And this opened up a whole new world, a world full of possibilities.

It all started with a football. *Ek American bhaiyya aaye the gaon mein – Franz bhaiyya.* He was living in Hutup – a small village in Jharkhand – because he wanted to see the 'real India'.

Franz used to play football with boys in the evenings and also taught a group of girls and boys English from time to time.

"I soon realised that the government schools these kids attend don't teach anything!"

Franz started a scholarship for 10 boys and girls, so they could attend private school. He also liked to chat with the children in *tooti-footi* Hindi and understand their life, their problems.

One of the girls in the scholarship program was 11-year-old Mansi. *Baaton baaton mein* Franz bhaiyya asked her, "What do you like to do in your free time?"

"I like to play football," she replied.

Franz was surprised. He had never seen any girls playing in the village.

When pressed, Mansi admitted, "No. I have never played ... *par main khelna chahti hoon.*"

"Will you play alone or do you have some friends who can join?"

"I will bring my friends," she said.

"Okay then, what time should we play?"

"At 4.30 in the morning," came the reply.

The next day, before dawn, a rag-tag bunch of girls assembled on a makeshift ground. They were in frocks, skirts and old salwars. All of them were barefoot.

When Franz signalled to begin the match, the girls ran onto the field in full josh. They kicked, they screamed, they laughed, tumbled and fell.

"I had never seen so much enthusiasm from the boys!"

When Franz organised a football tournament in the village, it was the girls who turned up in large numbers. The boys showed no interest.

"The boys wanted football jerseys and a fancy ball – the girls just wanted to play!"

So Franz decided to form a team and coach them. He had absolutely no idea what he was getting into. Girls in villages do not play football. *Sab ko pata hai ladke-ladki mein fark hota hai.*

Girls cook the food but they eat last. They clean up after everybody.

All boys go to school, but not all girls. They don't

really need to study.

All girls must be married quickly, before they bring 'shame' to the family.

So what if the husband is some alcoholic, good-for-nothing? These girls who came to play football would hardly be shocked – it was a daily tamasha in their families.

"*Roz shaam ko bapu sharaab peekar aatey hain aur maa ke saath maar-peet karte hain.*"

But for that hour-and-a-half on the field, all these troubles were left behind. No cooking, no cleaning. No taunting, no scolding.

School mein na sahi, ghar mein na sahi, at least there is one place where I can have some fun.

Playing football became the highlight of their day. And the girls came in droves. Each new player bringing friends with her.

Soon the villagers started taking notice. They sneered and passed comments.

"Where is she going, what does she do? *Bigad jayegi bachchi!*"

When some girls started wearing hand-me-down shorts, the boys thought it was funny.

"*Arey aur chhote kapde pehen le!*"

"*Khelna toh aata nahin, ladkon se barabari karne chali hain...*"

The girls felt humilated but kept silent. At least they had football to look forward to. But it wasn't easy to keep playing.

One day they came for practice to find the entire field had been tilled. It was a *banjar zameen*, never used for cultivation.

"*Sab hum ko rokne ka tareeka.*"

But instead of picking a fight, they simply shifted to another ground. Picked up a jhadu, swept the field, and started playing!

Franz believed in making the girls decision-makers from day one. And slowly the girls were growing in confidence. They decided everything in 'planning meetings', from the football practice schedule to what equipment and resources they needed.

But one day, the girls wrote down an unexpected 'demand': regular English classes.

And that's how extra classes were started for the Yuwa girls. Every day after practice.

If anyone had asked Kusum or Kiran or Shashi or

Khushi a few years ago – *"Aap bade hokar kya banna chahti ho"* – they would've had the same answer. "I want to be a nurse" or "I want to be a teacher".

But now they were realising that girls could do so much more. That having dreams and ambitions was good.

The girls came to play football every single day at 4.30 in the morning. They also started attending school regularly.

For the next three years, Franz worked tirelessly with the Yuwa girls. Slowly other likeminded people joined him. Interns and volunteers from all over the world came to help out for a few months at a time. Each of them played an important role in strengthening Yuwa. Like Anya Gupta, an MBA graduate from MIT, USA, who took over critical administrative work. And Pulkit, an IIT graduate, who helped design brochures and pamphlets for fundraising.

Some volunteers also became full-time members of the team. Rose, a young girl from Missouri, USA, came to Yuwa for a brief stint to teach the girls and coach football. She stayed on and is now the Yuwa school principal. Similarly, Niharika Baxla, a postgraduate in computer applications from BIT-Mesra, is the Child Development Officer, and is like an elder sister to the Yuwa girls.

The Yuwa staff knew that the girls had talent and determination. What they desperately needed was a platform to showcase it. So the girls started participating in tournaments, first at the school level, then state level and finally at the national level.

In 2013, Franz decided to enter the Yuwa team for the prestigious Gasteiz Cup – the all-woman under-14 football tournament held every year in Spain – and the Donosti Cup in San Sebastian, Spain.

The girls were super excited. *"Hamein videsh jaane ka mauka mil raha hai! Par decide kaise karenge ki kaun jayega?"* There were about 100 girls who came to play football regularly, but just 13 would be selected.

Franz chose an unusual way to pick the team. He asked the girls to rank each other on five values: Positivity, Honesty, Caring, Selflessness and Team Unity.

"Football toh sab khelte hain, magar achcha insaan kaun hai? Acchhi team unhi se banti hai."

One girl called Rinki was ranked #1 on every single value by every single player. She was made the team captain. Other team members were picked in a similar fashion.

"What I wanted most in the Yuwa team was a positive attitude and work ethic!"

As word about the trip to Spain spread in the village, so did the rumours. *"Ladkiyan hawaijahaaz mein baith kar videsh ja rahi hain."* Jealousy reared its ugly head.

They whispered, "That foreigner is taking your daughter outside the country – he will sell her there!"

Franz and his team visited the homes of these girls and convinced their parents to sign the required documents.

But the problems did not end there. The girls needed birth certificates to apply for their passport. When they visited the office the panchayat sevak refused to give them the documents.

At first he taunted them verbally, *"Tum itni chhoti aur weak ho; wahan haar jaogi!"*

Then he asked for a bribe but refused to give the certificates, even after they had paid up.

When the girls persisted, the clerk decided 'enough was enough'. He slapped one of the girls and told the others to pick up a *jhaadu* and start sweeping the floor.

The Yuwa staff and board members were furious. Something had to be done; this couldn't be tolerated. So Franz went to the Ranchi correspondent of the *Hindustan Times*. The issue came to the notice of higher authorities who leaned on the clerk. The girls got their birth certificates and their passports, and Franz rushed to New Delhi for the visas.

"The Spanish Consulate worked after hours to process the application..."

It was a photo finish as the players finally boarded their flight to Spain from Kolkata. The Yuwa team landed in the city of San Sebastian for the first tournament – the Donosti Cup. They were warmly welcomed and interviewed by local press, radio and television stations.

"One really touching moment was when a boys' team saw our girls in a public place and started clapping, chanting 'India, India'!"

"Ladka ho ya ladki, wahan koi farak nahin." It was a refreshing change and boosted team morale.

Yet, the tournament was a big challenge. The Yuwa girls had never played on grass or astroturf. In fact, they had no experience of playing on a full-size football field.

They lost 3-1 in their very first match against a team from Wisconsin, USA. But as the games continued, the tide turned.

In their next two matches against two teams from Spain, the girls played their hearts out and won. Unfortunately they lost after that.

But the fact that the girls had made it to the quarterfinals of an international tournament gave them the boost they needed. Franz had playfully nicknamed the Yuwa team 'The Supergoats' because they were fearless, ever ready to butt heads for what they wanted. And now the goats were coming into their own.

When the next tournament started, the *josh* of the Yuwa girls' team was unmatched. Yuwa placed third overall in the Gasteiz Cup, winning the bronze medal. When their name was announced, the girls ran into the dressing room and changed into traditional red and white sarees. And when they got down from the podium, they began the traditional 'jhumar' dance. They chanted:

"Yuwa yuwa hum hai yuwa, sab se juda;
Gendwa ko maarei, netwa ko phaade,
Mil ke bolo Jai Yuwa!"

Main un ladkiyon ko message dena chahti hoon jo school nahin jaati. Kripya karke school jaye aur apne life mein aagey badhe.
– Rinki, Yuwa Team Captain.

Everything had changed when they returned to the village. Parents proudly declared – "This is my daughter." *Log unko izzat ki nazar se dekhne lagey.*

Those who sneered at girls playing football now wanted to send their daughters to Yuwa. *Kya pata, uski bhi kismat khul jaaye?*

Today, there are 300 girls in the Yuwa program. They not only play football, they also attend the newly set-up Yuwa school. A very different school from the one the girls used to attend.

"The truth is, I never wanted to start a school. But it is the only way to give our girls the education they deserve."

The Yuwa school has an average of 15 students per class. English medium education with free bus and low fees. Yet, there was a lukewarm response.

"We told the parents that we won't beat your kids, but they couldn't understand that!"

They said, *"Maarenge nahin toh bachcha seekhega kaise…"*

Slowly, this mindset is changing. More and more girls want to join the Yuwa school. In fact, the plan is to build another school for 600 children.

The Yuwa team has also grown over the years. Now there are 10 full-time members and 27 part-time employees. A professional football coach has also been hired for the girls. Part of his job is to groom the next generation of coaches. Currently, 20 senior girls and five boys act as coaches for Yuwa's junior teams (and get paid for this work).

"Aagey jaakar yeh ek career path bhi ho sakta hai."

Yes, there are many paths beckoning these girls now. *Koi journalist banna chahti hai, toh koi pilot.* Rinki Kumari has even bigger ambitions. She now speaks English fluently and was invited to speak at TEDx in IIFT Delhi. Standing on stage, Rinki declared:

"When I grow up, I want to be a divorce lawyer. Many girls I know want to divorce their husbands because their husbands hurt them, drink alcohol and spend all the family's money on drinking or gambling. But women do not know how to get a divorce. I want to help women so they can be free to get a good job and save money for their future."

Rinki will not get married until she completes her education and gets a good job. The parents of Yuwa girls are asked to sign a 'bond' on stamp paper – so they cannot go back on their word.

"The girls today may still have to fight the same battles, but they are now better fighters."

The Yuwa girls have changed the rules in their village. Now a bright, new generation of girls are unafraid to say, *"Mujhe bhi jeeney do, aasmaan mein udane do. Sapna dekh rahi hoon, usey sach karne ki himmat hai!"*

My Choice

Usha Choudhary
Udaipur, Rajasthan

"You're a girl – tumhari zindagi ka maksad hai shaadi aur bacche." Usha Choudhary has devoted her life to one mission: to give the power of choice to women. The choice to study, the choice to work and the choice to marry when they want to.

"*Aate hi ladki paida kar di isne.*"

These were the words relatives uttered to her mother, when Usha Choudhary was born. For a girl was nothing but a burden in an orthodox Jat family in Rajasthan.

"*Dekhna, ab toh saat aur ladkiyan paida hogi. Parivaar mein line lag jayegi!*" they taunted.

It was only when her next child was a boy that Usha's mother felt secure, *ki "ab mujhe ghar se nahin nikalenge."*

Usha could not understand everything but she knew that her grandparents didn't give her the *laad-pyaar* they gave her brother.

Growing up, Usha also witnessed her mother being beaten by her alcoholic father. Many times, she would leave the house and go to her *maika* for a few days. *"Ki shayad mere jaane se kuch sudhar jayenge."*

The responsibility of taking care of her siblings fell on Usha's tender shoulders. *"Ek side pe exam ke liye padhti, aur dusri aur sab ke liye khaana banaati."*

Due to his drinking, Usha's father lost his job. So he opened a small tea stall to support them, while her mother worked as a labourer in cotton fields.

Even Usha and her younger brother had to start working. *"Hum padhai ke saath saath, khet me mummy ke saath mazdoori karte the."*

Despite having to work as labourers, she never gave up on her studies. That was when Usha first realised that, with determination, she could overcome any hurdle.

But in 10th standard, Usha's real awakening began. It started with when she, along with her family, went to visit her grandparents during the holidays.

One afternoon, while Usha was playing with her cousins, she saw that many of her relatives had come over. After two hours, the adults called her inside and made her sit with them.

"Aur achanak se meri maang bhar di, gehne-kapde de diye."

Usha was in a state of shock. The whole affair lasted only 10 minutes. Before she could make head or tail of what had happened, everyone had left.

Usha hadn't even seen her 'husband'. *Kisi ne bataaya ki woh army mein hai. Isiliye ladke ki ma ne maang bhar di.*

When she heard this, Usha began screaming her lungs out.

"Main shaadi nahin karoongi! Mujhe abhi padhna hai!"

No one paid attention to her. They thought she would fall in line in a few days.

When the family returned to Chittorgarh, Usha tried to talk to her parents. But they were not willing to listen.

"Manaa kiya toh koi aur rishta nahin aayega. Tere bhai-beheno ke baare me soch!"

But Usha refused to cooperate. Because of her zidd, the marriage never happened. At the same time – although she was so young – Usha decided that she must learn to be financially independent.

'Agar main kamaoongi toh mere saath zabardasti nahin ho sakti."

So, in 11th standard, Usha took up a job. First she began teaching nursery class children in her own school. Then she started tuitions for the children in her neighbourhood. Soon she also took up an admin job at a courier company.

Through all this, Usha continued her education by going to school in the evening, and then studying up to-post graduation via distance learning.

In those seven to eight years, from 11th standard to MA in Hindi Literature, Usha would leave home at 6 am and return at 10 pm. When everyone at home was asleep.

To avoid any unwanted male attention and to shut up the gossipmongers, she came up with a unique idea.

"Main kapde simple pehenti thi, baal mein tel, aur tight-tight choti banaati thi."

So that no one could say that Usha is not getting married because of an affair.

With hard work and sheer perseverance, Usha finally finished her MA. Over the years, she had nurtured a deep desire to do something for women. To become a social worker.

"But what exactly should I do?" she thought.

A like-minded friend suggested, *"Ek school kholte hai!"*

Usha liked this idea. So they opened a school in a Dalit neighbourhood in Chittorgarh. People said, *"Yeh kahan jaake school khola tumne!"*

But Usha and her friend Manju Joshi were unfazed. *"Jahan zaroorat lag rahi hai, hum wahin school kholenge."*

Usha worked tirelessly for three years to grow the school from one class, to a school with multiple divisions in each standard.

But still Usha did not feel fulfilled. Every now and then she would think to herself, *"Mujhe kuch aur karna hai. Magar kya?"*

The answer came in the form of a classified ad in the local newspaper: 'NGO working with widows and tribal women is looking for field staff.'

Usha could hardly control her excitement. *"Arre, yeh toh meri pasand ka kaam hai. Yeh toh main kar sakti hoon!"*

So Usha appeared for the interview at Astha Sansthan. There were many more experienced candidates, but when it was her turn, the interviewer was bowled over by her honesty and enthusiasm.

"Maine imaandari se kaha mere paas experience nahin hai. Magar kuch karna chahti hoon. Mahilaon ki zindagi badalne ka irada hai."

She got the job!

Usha was over the moon. But there was one catch – it was in Udaipur. How would she convince her parents to let her move there?

But this was her once-in-a-lifetime opportunity, and she couldn't afford to waste it. After a lot of convincing, Usha finally got her way.

In Udaipur, Usha threw herself into work. Day and night, she was either at the office or out in the 'field'. In fact, her coordinator had to tell her, *"Chheh mahine ho gaye hai aur tumne chutti nahin li. Ab tum ghar jao!"*

But there was no stopping Usha. She was there to 'live' her job, not just do it.

At Astha Sansthan, Usha was involved in many campaigns – from helping single women and widows learn about their rights to promoting adult literacy.

Finally, Usha knew what the purpose of her life was. She resolved not to get married. So that the demands of a family and a husband would not get in the way of following her passion.

But at home, the pressure was mounting. Her mother made emotional appeals, rational appeals and finally, there were loud and angry words.

Usha repeatedly tried to explain her reasons: *"Shaadi nahin karna meri 'choice' hai."* Respect it! But her protests fell on deaf ears. Finally, one day, her brother stepped in.

"Mummy, aap kyun har baar didi ke saath ladayi karte hain?"

"Isne shaadi nahin ki, toh tum logon ki shaadi kaise hogi?"

"Agar shaadi nahin hogi toh koi baat nahin. Hum chaaron kunware reh jayenge, magar didi ko mat pareshaan karo."

Usha's mother fell silent. She understood that *bhai-behen ek the*, and nothing was going to stop them from following their hearts.

Finally Usha's mother quietly accepted her daughter's choice.

Usha continued to work at Astha for five years. During this time, she got incredible opportunities to attend conferences and trainings around the world. Where she met passionate, like-minded people. During intense discussions, they would often conclude that working with the 'youth' will bring about the most change in society.

Then one day Usha's friend, Kiran, and Yogesh (her colleague from Astha Sansthan) approached her out of the blue. *"Chalo apan youth ke liye kaam karte hai."*

Kiran had met a group of young girls who had prepared a play to fund drought-relief efforts. But their parents had forbidden them from performing in public.

Usha, Yogesh, Kiran and another friend Rajkumar immediately went to Barmer to meet the girls.

"Hamaare saath hamesha aise hi hota hai. Koi kuch karne nahin deta. Didi, aap kuch help karo."

Usha could relate to their story as if it were her own.

So the four of them took matters into their own hands. They collected all the girls and sat in the small room. With a marker, she wrote the 'mission plan' on the door.

"Ladkiyon ke saath teen din tak hum baithe. Tab Vikalp naam nikla."

Vikalp means 'alternative'. A new way of thinking, where girls can live freely.

"Aur daud pade hum sab race mein, bina chappal aur joote."

Using their own money, Usha, Kiran and Yogesh went on a 'research' trip around India. They returned with renewed *josh* and excitement – to do something.

But they soon realised that the biggest problem was funds – they didn't have any. So one of them would have to take up a job while the others would run Vikalp.

For two years, Usha worked in different NGOs. Whatever salary she earned, she gave away most of it to Vikalp every month. In the meantime, Yogesh was working with girls in about 20–25 villages in the Barmer *jilla*.

In her holidays, Usha would return to Barmer and roam the village roads on a black motorcycle. Girls would often stare – they had never seen anyone like her before!

This *didi* with her short boycut hair and bold attitude.

Slowly, they gathered the courage to talk to her. And Usha would try to get them to start coming to the youth resource centre started by Vikalp. The centre had books, magazines and newspapers, also art and craft workshops.

Kuch padenge, samjhenge tabhi toh mentality bhi badlegi.

Finally, Usha quit her job and joined Vikalp full time. By this time, well-wishers were coming forward with funding.

"Humne logon ko bol diya tha ki hum paise nahin lenge. Aapko madad karni hai toh aap bike mein petrol dalwa sakte hai, t-shirt ka paisa de sakte hai, ya poster printing ke paise de sakte hai."

The girls who had once eyed Usha from a distance started participating in campaigns. They would make educational comics and posters and go from village to village shouting slogans. One of their campaigns was called *'Apni Dikri Ro Haq'*, or 'Our Daughter's Right', an awareness bike rally where 80 young men and women participated in three districts in Rajasthan.

Ladkiyon ko jab apne pankhon par udne ka mauka milega tab hi samaaj mein barabari aayegi.

"Woh campaign hamaara bahut successful tha."

One man even came up and said that, despite the pressure to have a son, he had decided to be content with his two daughters.

The campaign lasted for five to six days. But it was a turning point for both Usha and Vikalp.

A group of 8th pass girls who had participated in the rally gathered around Usha and started to cry.

"Humein ghar nahin jaana," they wailed.

Usha was stumped. *"Kyun nahin jaogi?"*

"Hum padhna chahte hai. Abhi hum ghar gaye toh hamaari shaadi ho jayegi."

Usha was shocked. *"Mujhe aisa laga jaise meri life ne wapis se mujhe current maari – jo itne saal pehle mere saath hua, yeh wohi ho raha hai."*

In that group, some were already married, while others were soon to be engaged. So Usha promised them: *"Hum aapko padhayenge aur shaadi nahin hone denge. Jinka bal vivah ho gaya hai, unko sasural nahin jaane denge."*

In the backward *jilla* of Barmer, this promise was not easy to make. But from that day on, Vikalp's focus turned towards the eradication of child marriage.

First, they did a survey of all the girls who lived in the village to see how many were still in school. *Aur agar dropout hai toh iska bal vivah se kya connection hai.*

"Phir samajh aya ki agar shiksha badhegi toh bal vivah ghatenge."

At the time, the villages did not have any school beyond 8th standard. And parents were not ready to send their daughters far away to study at the government high school. In fact, the girls who had approached Usha had left studies two–three years ago.

Usha and her colleagues had to counsel and convince the parents. They were thus able to enroll 50–60 girls as private candidates for the state board exams.

The next problem was – who was going to guide them? Usha begged the village teacher to take extra tuitions for the girls. But she did not agree.

So the Vikalp team motivated the boys, who were

part of their campaigns, to help their sisters. Luckily this plan worked. And slowly, *badlaav ane laga.*

Ek instance tha – ek bhai-behen the. Both were in the 10th standard. The boy had got a second-class pass, while the girl had got a first-class pass. Despite that, the parents wanted to get her married.

The boy was associated with the Vikalp youth group. He told his parents, *"Main padh ke kya karoonga? Didi ke saath aap meri bhi shaadi karwa do."*

The parents were speechless, but in this way, the girl's marriage was stopped. The siblings were later sent to Barmer to pursue further studies.

Vikalp's efforts to educate young boys and girls were starting to show results.

The group of 10 girls who Usha had promised to help got permission to stay at the Vikalp office for four months. The Vikalp team organised coaching classes, life skills workshops and movie screenings.

The girls learnt a lot and Usha could see that they had become more confident. But when the exam results came, she was shattered. All 10 girls had failed!

Yeh kaise hua? Ab kya kahenge saare parents ko?

The team's excitement died down. The girls became

quiet while the parents were furious. For two–three months, Vikalp stopped all activities.

They knew that it was time to introspect. To find out what went wrong.

Finally they realised that the girls had left school a while ago; they could not cope with the workload. But one failure is not the end of the world. *Let us try again.*

So they returned to the field and once again convinced parents to fill the forms. More than 100 girls enrolled. This time, they would study in their own homes.

But the girls had a different plan in mind…

One day, Kabbu, Hathu, Sashi and all their friends marched into the Vikalp premises, climbed up the stairs and locked themselves in a room.

Usha and her colleague Kusum stared at each other. *Arre yeh ladkiyan kyun aayi hai?*

The girls said, *"Hamein padhna hai, aur aap hi ke saath. Hum ghar wapas nahin jayenge!"*

It was a day of great pride for Usha. After so many struggles, the girls had become confident and outspoken. They were fighting for what they wanted.

So Usha promised them once again. *"Hum aapko ghar nahin bhejenge."*

And this time, all 10 girls passed!

Today, many of these girls have finished their BA or B.Ed. They are employed as teachers, nurses and Anganwadi workers. And none of them got married before the age of 18.

Over the past 10 years, there has been a sea change in Barmer *jilla*. Over 8,000 girls have been saved from child marriages, 10,000 girls have enrolled for higher education, and 1,600 domestic violence survivors have been counselled. Usha and the dedicated Vikalp team have stepped in countless times, convincing parents, educating girls and boys, and spreading awareness through rallies and campaigns.

Vikalp has also educated hairdressers, decorators and makeup artists who once catered to child marriages, to stop providing services to them. Now many of them alert Usha when they hear of a child marriage in a village.

Usha lives by one rule: *"Agar meri zindagi badli hai toh meri zimmedari hai ki main dusron ki zindagi badloon."*

And slowly but surely, she is changing the world around her. And creating a new tribe of change-makers.

Dukh to Sukh

Meena Lahre
Korba, Chattisgarh

Husband drinks, wife suffers – yeh ghar ghar ki kahaani hai. But Meena Lahre refused to accept this. Apni soch aur samajhdari se, woh puri family ko line pe le aayi.

Early one morning, Meena Lahre's phone rang. On the other end was her mother. *"Mujhe yahaan se le jaa,"* she cried. *Bas. Usi waqt Meena ne tay kar liya ki ab aur sehna nahin.*

In the small town of Korba, Chattisgarh, Meena had grown up knowing only one truth: *Aadmi zulm karte hai, aur auratein chup chap sehti hai. Maayka ho ya sasural, dono parivar mein izzat nahin milti.*

Growing up, Meena's family was like many others in her community. The men were into womanizing, sharaab and maar-peet. Meena's father had a very bad reputation. *"Kahin sharab ya ladki dekha toh mann phisal jaata tha unka."*

When she was five years old, Meena's father brought home a second wife. Meena's mother accepted this quietly. *Aur karein bhi kya?* She was financially and socially dependent on her husband. But Meena knew that this was fundamentally wrong.

The situation didn't improve even after the second wife left their house. Meena's father would still flirt with other women and even shamelessly ask his wife to help him. *"Koi aurat unko pasand aa jaye toh meri maa ko bolte the, tu usko mere liye leke aaja. Aise hi seedha seedha."*

He didn't spare Meena either. When she was only eight, her father sent her to buy alcohol for him. In that shady theka, Meena was exposed to things no girl her age should have to go through. *"Kabhi kuch bolte the, kabhi chhoote the. Woh sab kaam jo ek ladki ko shobha nahi deta uss umar mein, woh sab karwa te the."*

When she turned 15, her family started talking about getting her married. Her older sister had been married off at 13 and everyone was now worried about Meena's *badhti umar*. No one paid attention to the fact that her elder sister was tortured and beaten by her abusive husband. *Yeh toh har ghar ki kahaani thi.*

So teenage Meena was sent off to her mausi's home in BALCO. Her aunt was supposed to keep her safe and find a good *rishta*. Instead, Meena became her mausa's prey. *"Mere mausaji ka bhi character theek nahi tha. Unka bhi neeyat kharab ho gaya mere pe. Toh unhone bhi mujhko molest karne ki koshish ki."*

This incident traumatised Meena. She couldn't concentrate properly on her studies and hence failed 10th standard. When she told her mother about what had happened, she was told to keep quiet.

Meena's mother was afraid that this assault would

cause a rift in the family. And who would believe the word of a young girl.

Bas ab toh shaadi karwa kar Meena ko apne ghar bhej do.

So, the hunt for a boy for Meena began again. This time, Meena was introduced to a family who liked her. Their son had a reputation of being awaara, par *"family accha tha, toh haan bol di"*. Like the other women in her family, Meena knew that she was going to face the same problems. Her husband was a *sharaabi, juaari* and came home very late every night. Meena became a mother of two daughters soon after marriage, but her husband had taken up no responsibilities of having a family. *Agar kabhi kuch bola toh maar peet bhi dete the.*

But Meena was strong. *Woh jaanti thi ki apna jeevan khud hi sudhaarna tha.* Fortunately Meena's *sasuraal* was very supportive. Her father-in-law knew how much his son's actions hurt Meena. So they decided *ki bete ko sudhaar ne ka ek hi raasta hai: ghar se bahar nikalo aur apne pairon pe khud khade rehne do.*

Jab support system nahin raha, toh Meena ke husband ko akal aayi. Those were tough years for Meena. The family had no money, and Meena had to often go back to her in-laws' home to feed the kids.

"Ma, bolne wale bolte rahenge. Jo bolta hai, woh khilata nahin!"

After three years, things finally started looking up for Meena. Her husband became friends with a Zilla Adhyaksh called S B Kashyap, who brought them from the *basti* to the BJP Union office quarter.

And when the Nagar Nigam's seat was reserved for Scheduled Caste candidates, S B Kashyap suggested that Meena fight the elections. Now her husband began supporting her too.

"Bhagyavash, kismet se kahiye," Meena ne seat jeet li.

For the first time in her life, Meena felt respected. In a way that neither her mother nor her elder sister had ever experienced in all their years.

The first thing she did was solve her domestic problems. *"Mister ko bole ki aap bahar drink karna chhod do. Ab main Paarishad hoon, izzat hai, aap bahar drink mat karo itna."* Thankfully, her husband agreed.

Now the daily shouting, fighting and beating came to a stop. *"Aur ghar waale, sasuraal waale sab kehne lage ki beta tumhari wajah se hi yeh sudhra hai."* Even other women with alcoholic husbands came to her for help. She counselled them, and helped them reach out to NGOs dedicated to fighting alcoholism.

But for Meena, her biggest achievement was helping her mother.

After her husband left her, her mother was harassed by her *beta* and *bahu. "Bhabhi humaari jo thi, khoob torture kiya maa ko. Sabke liye khaana lagati, par unko nahi poochti ki khaya ya nahi. Uske kapde alag se usi se dhulwati thi. Nana prakaar se torture karti thi."*

When she couldn't take it anymore, Meena's mother secretly called her. It was very early in the morning. Everyone at home was sleeping.

On the phone she cried her heart out. She said after 50 years of living like this, she couldn't take it anymore. Meena didn't think twice. She left right away for her brother's house to fetch her mother.

By evening, her mother had settled into her new home. Neither her husband nor her in-laws objected. *Par Meena ki ma beti ke ghar rehne me hich-kicha rahi thi. Kyunki log kya kahenge.*

After her mother shared her doubts, Meena had only

one answer for her: *"Ma, bolne wale bolte rahenge. Jo bolta hai, woh khilata nahin!"*

Meena's confidence convinced her mother. Now she has finally found a happy home. *Jahaan shanti hai, izzat hai aur pyaar.*

"Abhi toh woh mere Mister ko hi beta maanti hai. Kabhi ladai hota hai toh unke side ho jaati hai. Meri saas ke saath bhi dosti se hi hai."

Meena's courage has finally broken the vicious cycle of abuse in her family. In a world where parents think their sons will become their *budhape ki laathi, ek beti ne apni aur apni ma ki zindagi badal di.*

Meri Mom

Chhaya Solanki
Chandkheda, Gujarat

"Widows are bad luck – shaadi mein mat bulao." When Chhaya Solanki's widowed mother could not to be part of her wedding, Chhaya decided to stand up for her. Because mom ke haqq ke liye ladne se zyaada kya important hai?

Chhaya Solanki tore open the plastic and felt the soft fabric of her wedding sari. "I am the luckiest girl in the world!" she thought to herself.

Soon, very soon, she would marry the man of her dreams.

But behind her broad smile was a story of struggle. Her family had not been easy to convince.

"Horoscope match nahi ho raha, teri zindagi mein problem aa jayenge, yeh woh…"

Her mother had agreed to the match but her brothers were creating problems.

"Love marriage matlab pata nahi kya tha unke liye…"

Bhai log had even called Ajay and threatened him with grave consequences if he didn't back out. Finally, Chhaya mustered the courage to tell her brothers that she would not bow to their pressure.

"Unse keh diya maine, shaadi karoongi toh inse hi karoongi. Inse pyaar kiya hai, doosre se shaadi kaise kar loon?"

Haar ke, Chhaya's brothers gave their consent – planning and preparations for the wedding began.

"Finally, itna sab ke baad, meri shaadi ho rahi hai!" Only Chhaya knew how much that beautiful sari

meant. She was going to be the happiest bride in all of Chandkheda.

Chhaya looked up and saw her mother standing at the door with a sheepish little smile. "See my lovely sari!" the bride-to-be exclaimed.

The expression on her mother's face changed.

"Teri shaadi waale kapde mujhse door hi rakh, don't bring the sari near me," said her mother and turned her face away.

"Matlab kyun? … Kyun nahi choo sakti, wo toh batao!"

The matter-of-fact reply shocked Chhaya.

"I am a widow. It will not be auspicious."

That's when it hit Chhaya. As a widow, her mother would not be allowed to take part in any of the marriage rituals. She would not apply *haldi* during the peethi ceremony. She would not receive the groom and his *baaraat*. In fact, she would not even be allowed near the *mandap*.

Basically, she wasn't allowed to do any of the activities that a mother has a right to in a Gujarati wedding.

Her brother-in-law and his wife would perform the *kanyadaan*.

"Papa toh hain nahi, Mom bhi meri shaadi mein

shameel nahin ho sakti."

What irked Chhaya the most was that her mother herself had accepted this.

"Wo khud yeh sab manna nahi chahti thi, andar se. Yeh sach hai. Unko bhi achcha nahi lagta, lekin kya kare? Bole reeti riwaz hai, yeh hai, wo hai, karna padta hai."

She had become so used to sacrifice that she had accepted these rules without question. All in the name of samaaj, which continued to treat widows badly without question or comment.

In fact, the Wanker sub-caste, which both Chhaya and Ajay belong to, is not economically or educationally backward. Ajay points out, "Many are very well educated – they are doctors, engineers. But still their thoughts are same."

Chhaya remembers how her mother was made to sweep the village street right after the death of her father. She had to do this every morning for the entirety of the mourning period.

"Bole unke pair ke nishan wapas aate hai. Toh phir achcha nahi hota, is liye jhadu lagwate hain."

There are many such *niyams* of the *samaaj*, which only serve to shame widows.

The widow is made to take a bath outside the house.

Her bangles are broken in public by striking a rock on her arms.

Usually there is bleeding, and in some cases, injury. *"Uske haath pe lagti hai, nahi lagti hai wo kisiko parwah nahi hai."*

Chhaya was only 21 years old then, and had not raised her voice in protest. But, she did resist in her own small ways.

Her mother was not supposed to change her clothes for 12 days. *"Hygiene ki toh fikar hi nahi thi kisiko, bolte paap lagega, yeh … woh…"*

With the help of a sympathetic relative, Chhaya made sure that every night her mother wore a fresh saree. *"Waapis subah woh pehle waali saree pehna dete the, kisike uthne se pehle."*

Chhaya wasn't proud that she had to be so meek in her rebellion but she knew it was a sensitive time. Anything she said would have been taken very negatively.

People would say: *"Baap mar gaya hai, par yeh duniya ko sudhaarne ka jhanda leke ghoom rahi hai."*

What's more, they were dependent on the extended family to properly conduct the last rites. In that situation, it was not wise to oppose these things openly.

But now, things had changed. At least, that's what Chhaya believed. And so she decided that it was high time she raised her voice against this injustice.

"Main toh chahti thi ki har rasm mein meri mom hissa le." But she soon realised that she could not change the age-old mindset overnight.

"Sab bole, tu bahut jiddi hai, tu yeh hai. Bahut saare log bahut saari bate banane lage." Even her mother was not ready to break all shackles.

"Tu yeh sab mat kar. Sab log wapas chale jayenge, koi saath khada nahi hoga, yeh ... woh... Phir kaise hogi shaadi?" No matter what she asked her mother to do, Chhaya did not get much support from her. She wanted to take part, but was too afraid of defying the other members in the family.

On one point though, Chhaya was firm. It would be her mother who would welcome the groom into the ceremony by putting the teeka on his forehead.

"Main ek hi unki ladki hu, akeli. Unka hi haq banta hai."

The teeka ceremony is one of the most significant and auspicious rituals in a Gujarati wedding. When

"Kisi ka pati marjaye, ismein widow ki thodi galti hai. Usko kyon itna torture kiya jata hai? Yeh sawaal main sab se poochna chahti hoon."

relatives came to know of Chhaya's stand, there was an uproar.

"Paap lagega, tera pati bhi mar jayega, lakhon problems aayengi tere life mein, yeh woh."

Chhaya told everyone that she didn't care. She didn't believe in any of this.

But she realised that she couldn't drive this point through by herself. Her plan would succeed only if she had Ajay's support.

She called and asked him pointblank if he had a problem with her widowed mother welcoming him at the wedding. Ajay remembers that he was completely okay with it.

"*Actually, meri khud ki mom bhi widow hai*, my father died 25 years back. When I was five years old. *So, maine bhi yeh dekha … iss samaj mein kya kya sehan karna padta hai*. Same with my mother-in-law *aur* with my mother."

And so it was decided.

Chhaya told everyone in the family that if anyone other than her mother came out to welcome the groom, the *baaraat* would go back. Was she actually prepared for that to happen? Or was it just an empty threat?

Ajay was confident that this threat would be taken seriously. The mere thought of a groom returning from the *mandap* was too big a stigma for any family!

Chhaya hoped Ajay's conviction was right. Somewhere inside, she had her doubts. And on the day of the marriage, her fears started coming true.

When Chhaya was done with her bridal makeup, she noticed that something was wrong with the preparation of the welcome *thaali*.

Her mother wasn't touching the *thaali* at all – everything was being arranged by her *chachi*. She understood immediately what was happening.

These people were thinking it was one big bluff.

"Itna bada apshagun hai. Baaraat thodi waapis jayegi." In that moment, she knew what she had to do. If she did not intervene now, her mother would never get what she deserved.

She gathered everyone and declared that if her mother wasn't allowed to welcome the groom, she would not sit in the *mandap*.

People were already exasperated with her. Now, they forgot all civilities and said all sorts of horrible things about Chhaya and her mother.

"Teri mom jo hai, wo koi nayi widow bani hai kya? Yeh wo, bahut saara sunaya mujhe."

Things were not going in her favour, but Chhaya didn't lose hope. She was firm about what she wanted.

Seeing that Chhaya would not change her mind, her relatives finally agreed to let her have her way. *"Bole ki thik hai tu hai, teri problem hai, tu solve kar le."*

Ajay remembers how he smiled when he saw his mother-in-law with the *teeka thaali* and a lot of happy tears. He also remembers how the rest of the *biradari* did not share his happiness.

Mahaul kuch thanda tha. Far too many people had been offended and many of them were holding a grudge. How could a widow defy convention like this?

It was a small victory but an important victory.

Today, seven years later, that one brave step by Chhaya is still talked about at weddings. Most people still point fingers but a few have embraced new ideas.

Love marriages have become more acceptable, thanks to the happy example of Chhaya and Ajay. More and more widows are coming out of the shadows and participating in celebrations.

Ajay is sad that his mother could not come with the *baaraat* but that too is slowly changing.

Chhaya doesn't consider herself to be anything out of the ordinary. *"Mere ghar mein hua, toh maine kiya."*

She never thought of herself as a social reformer. But when the injustice was in front of her eyes, with her own mother, how could she simply accept it?

In her own circle and *samaaj*, Chhaya exerts a quiet influence. She wants people to think about what they say and be more sensitive about how they treat widows.

"Kisika pati marjaye, ismein widow ki thodi galti hai. Usko kyon itna torture kiya jata hai? Yeh sawaal main sab se poochna chahti hoon."

For it is when we start looking inwards, that we will find the path of truth. Where the mark of *sindoor* is but a label. Created by man, not sanctioned by God.

Chhaya dreams of the day when her mother will wear colourful *sarees* again.

When she will walk on the street with dignity and respect.

No different from anyone else.

Mission Possible

Rabiya Khan
Indore, Madhya Pradesh

"You are not normal – tum kuch nahin kar sakogi." Log aisa kehte the, magar Rabiya's parents brought her up to believe that anything is possible. As long as you are willing to struggle for it. For your own good, and for others.

"Jab main chhoti thi mera vision loss ho gaya tha."

Rabiya Khan was the youngest of four siblings, the apple of her father's eye. When she was one-and-a-half years old, the family realised "something is wrong". They took her from one doctor to another but finally had to accept – "Rabiya is born blind".

Nasir Khan ran a successful transport business and he believed in one thing – every problem in life has a solution.

"Rabiya dekh nahin sakti toh kya hua, usey zindagi ki har khushi haasil ho sakti hai."

First and foremost, she would get a good education. Initially, Rabiya attended a blind school where all subjects were taught in Braille. But when she was in 6th standard, her father decided to enrol her in Sanyogitagang (Jagdale) Higher Secondary School, Indore. A school for normal children.

Badi minnat ke baad principal ne blind student ko admission diya. But Rabiya worked twice as hard as the regular students and managed to cope.

"*Hamesha meri thinking thi ki main sabse equal rehna chahti hoon.* I don't want any special treatment."

Since she could not see the blackboard, Rabiya

worked out a method to take notes. She would borrow notebooks from friends and ask her sister to dictate the lessons. Rabiya then wrote down everything in Braille and studied it.

After passing 10th standard with the help of an exam writer, Rabiya joined Islamia Karimia Girls Higher Secondary School. During this time she also developed a fascination for computers. Taking special permission, Rabiya attended computer classes at the Blind School for Boys. But it was her brother Juned who really helped her to understand many concepts.

"Woh mujhe poora screen samjhaate the, ki kahan kya likha hai."

With the help of the JAWS software, which converts text to speech, Rabiya could operate the computer independently.

"Computer se maine bahut kuch seekha. Mujhe ek nayi hobby mil gayi."

Now came the time to choose a career. Rabiya's dream was to become a doctor but this was not possible for a blind person. She could not do 'practicals'.

"Maine socha … jo nahin ho sakta usko chhodo, jo hai uske saath aagey badho."

Rabiya decided to pursue law. But instead of BA-LLB (which would take six years), she wanted to enrol for the five-year law course directly after 12th.

Initially, she was refused a seat due to her disability. The HOD said, *"Prime Minister bhi nahin karwa sakte tumhara admission."*

Rabiya's father said, "The rule says that she is eligible – you will have to grant her admission."

Due to her persistence and insistence, Rabiya ultimately joined the Faculty of Law, Devi Ahilya Vishwavidyalaya, Indore. Rabiya enjoyed college life like any other girl of her age.

"Mujhe dress up hone ka bada shawk hai. Apne kapdon ka choice main khud karti hoon!"

Rabiya's family never made her wear a burkha. But they were devout Muslims who observed Ramzan and prayed five times a day. During Ramzan, the family recited verses of the Quran.

Rabiya used to listen to an audio version of the Holy Book but her heart longed to read it.

"Magar Arabic-Braille language mein Quran hamare India mein available nahin thi."

After a lot of inquiries, Rabiya learnt that a Braille

version of the Quran had been printed in Karachi. But ordering a book from Pakistan was cumbersome and expensive. And when it arrived several months later, there was a new problem.

Rabiya had learnt English and Hindi in Braille but she could not follow Arabic in Braille. Neither could she find anyone in Indore city who could be of help.

"Phir humne mind lagaya ki Aligarh Muslim University mein zaroor koi professor hoga."

Rabiya and her parents made three trips to Aligarh but each time they were turned away. The officials were rude and refused to even give an appointment. Day after day, they waited outside the building. Every evening, bade sir would walk past them, get inside his car and drive away. *Jaise ki yeh log koi hain hi nahin.*

Until Rabiya could take it no longer. She ran after him and cried out forcefully, *"Excuse me, aap ko do minute meri baat sunani hogi!"*

That's how Rabiya finally got a hearing. The university said it could arrange for a tutor, but she would have to arrange her own accommodation. Rabiya's father immediately booked a room in Hotel Gulmurg and agreed to stay back – as long as required.

"Maine wahan do mahine bahut mehnat se padhaai ki."

When she returned to Indore, Rabiya could read Arabic in Braille. She continued her Arabic studies, along with the study of law.

The following year, Rabiya's family decided to undertake the Haj pilgrimage. All of them filled the required forms and were busy making preparations.

"Main badi excited thi ki mujhe bhi yeh chance mil raha hai."

But Rabiya was in for a rude shock. The State Haj Committee sent her a letter saying: "Your application has been rejected." They said there is a rule: 'Blind pilgrims are not allowed in Mecca'.

Being a student of law, Rabiya asked to see the proof.

"Agar aisa koi rule hai toh aap mujhe uski copy dikha dijiye."

The committee took her lightly, after all she was a girl and she was blind – *kya kar legi? Unhe pata nahin tha ki Rabiya jhukne wali nahi hai.*

Rabiya decided to take the help of a senior advocate who took up public interest litigation. Advocate Satpal Anand sent a four-line 'attention letter' to the state and central Haj committee. At the same time, Rabiya also wrote an email to President Pratibha Patil, the Chairperson of the Haj Committee of India, and to Member of Parliament Mrs Mohsina Kidwai.

"Baat foreign ministry tak pahunch gayi aur aakhir mujhe permission mil gayi!"

Rabiya completed the pilgrimage without any problem. Her heart was full of gratitude and she thought to herself, "I have so much financial and moral support from my family. But what about other blind boys and girls?"

She had fulfilled all her desires – whether learning computers or studying law or reading the Quran in Arabic-Braille. But everyone was not so lucky.

"Maine socha ki blinds ke liye ek centre hona chahiye."

When she proposed this idea to her father, he said – *Accha hai, let us do it.* With the help of Professor Halim Khan (Secretary of Islamic Karimia Society in Indore), the Kwality Education Society for the Blind came into being. The centre began functioning from a room in the school itself.

The question was – how to find students? With the help of a list taken from the social justice and empowerment ministry, Rabiya and her father went door-to-door.

"Blind ki family ko samjhaya, motivate kiya ki unhe kuch seekhne ke liye hamare paas bhejo."

Rabiya herself was in her third year of college. But she somehow found time to manage her studies as well as the centre. And her efforts have borne fruit.

Today, more than 25 students regularly visit the Madrasa Noor Research Institute for the Blind, managed by the Kwality Education Society.

Taufeeq has come all the way from Jabalpur to learn Braille. And Shoaib, who lost his eyesight in an accident last year, says Rabiya ma'am is a very good teacher.

"Ma'am bahut friendly hain aur koi bhi problem ho, usko handle karna hamein seekha deti hain."

Tanish Srivastava is a bright boy who used to study in a blind school. Due to Rabiya's efforts, he was accepted in a normal school, where he is performing well.

"Bachcha padhaai mein itna acchha hai ki wahan sab log bahut khush hain."

Many students came to the centre to learn Arabic in Braille. But there was one big problem – where to get copies of the Quran in Braille? There was still no

"Internet se mera friend circle duniyabhar mein ho gaya hai. Unse maine bahut kuch seekha hai!"

edition available in India. And importing the books from Pakistan or Saudi Arabia was expensive.

That's when Rabiya realised there was only one solution – to convert the Quran into Arabic-Braille right here in India.

"Phir maine iss cheez pe work karna chalu kiya."

Initially Rabiya thought of scanning each page and converting the text to Braille using software. Then she tried to download the file and convert it. But none of these shortcuts worked.

The entire work had to be done manually – typing the Arabic words and converting them to Braille using the Duxbury translation software.

"Kisi tarah rasta jod liya magar kaam bahut difficult tha!"

Many a day Rabiya would come straight from college, or even exams, and spend six to eight hours at the computer. Ultimately, she decided to take a one-year break to focus on the conversion project. After 10 months of tireless efforts and with help from some of her students, Rabiya was able to compile 30 chapters of the Quran in Arabic-Braille and print them in six volumes.

"Large scale production ke liye hamein funds ki zaroorat hai."

At the same time, Rabiya is completing her LLB and plans to fill the form for LLM. She has also got a part-time job at Devi Ahilya Vishwavidyalaya where she trains blind students to pass the CCA exam (Certificate in Computer Applications). So far, she has trained more than 50 students. And all these activities keep her busy throughout the day.

"Free rehna mujhe pasand nahin, apna busy schedule mujhe pasand hai!"

Rabiya does take a break now and then by liking or commenting on Facebook or chatting on WhatsApp. In fact, she now has friends not only in India but all over the world: in Russia, Australia, USA and Africa.

"Internet se mera friend circle duniyabhar mein ho gaya hai. Unse maine bahut kuch seekha hai!"

Rabiya wants to share everything she has learnt with more and more blind students. She wants to expand the centre, provide hostel facilities, latest techonology and many other services.

As she is now 25 years of age, there is some talk of getting married and 'settled'. Rabiya is open to it. But she has told her family to look for an educated man who is also blind.

"Mera life partner aisa chahti hoon jis ke saath meri understanding ban sakti hai."

Isn't that what every girl wants?

Rabiya has struggled a lot to lead a 'normal' life. *But problem kis ki zindagi mein nahin hai?*

Apni problem mein na phanso, us sey lado.

For no problem is bigger than you, your spirit, your commitment and confidence!

Ma ka Pyaar

Shital Bhatkar
Mumbai, Maharashtra

"Mere saath aisa kyun hua... Shital Bhatkar's two-year-old son was diagnosed with a deadly disease. She could have crumbled, but instead she chose to fight. For a mother's love is deep and her heart is strong – it must go on."

Aarya was born on 4 May 2008 to Shital and Vikrant Bhatkar. *Ek pyaari beti ke baad ek cute beta – Shital ki chhoti si family complete ho gayi.*

"Right from birth, he had those big, beautiful eyes."

Shital could hardly contain her happiness. She had grown up picturing a typical happy family – husband, kids and a beautiful, cosy home. When her elder daughter, Prachiti, was born, Shital had willingly given up her job at IndusInd Bank to care for her. To run the house and run behind her kids.

From the outside everything looked perfect. But underneath, worry was eating away at Shital.

It started with the nightmares when she was pregnant. "I was continuously feeling like something is wrong, something is wrong." And no matter what she did, she couldn't shake this feeling off.

The baby was born without complications. But he was not developing normally. At one-and-a-half years of age, Aarya had still not started walking.

The paediatrician told her it's nothing – "Some babies take longer to walk, *hota hai.*" Shital tried to relax but her motherly instinct said – 'something is off'.

Finally, one day, the doctor said, "Okay, speak to Dr Brijesh Udani, he is a renowned neurologist. He'll find out if something is wrong."

Shital heaved a sigh of relief. Finally, she would get some answers. Shital and Vikrant sought an immediate appointment but the doctor was super-busy. He was able to meet them only three months later.

When Dr Udani checked Aarya, worry marked his face. "Aarya is not letting me touch his abdomen. Put him to sleep so I can examine him properly."

Shital and Vikrant anxiously sat in the waiting area for the next few hours. When the last patient had left, Dr Udani called them in again.

This time he examined Aarya thoroughly. Finally, he looked up and faced the parents. His eyes were sad, his face tired.

"Mr and Mrs Bhatkar, I am sorry to inform you … Aarya is suffering from 'Storage Disorder'."

In layman terms, this meant that Aarya's body was incapable of breaking down lipids like fat and cholesterol. So they would start building up on the body's essential organs like the spleen, liver, lungs and brains.

"In the long run, this usually leads to complete organ failure."

The diagnosis was devastating. There was virtually no hope, but still, Shital and Vikrant sought a second and third opinion. All the doctors agreed – the first step was to diagnose which type of Storage Disorder Aarya suffered from. Some types were curable. There was a slim chance that Aarya could be saved.

But finding out would not be easy. A patch of Aarya's skin would have to be sent to the only testing centre in the world in Netherlands. The centre was already backed up with cases.

"It took almost five months for us to get the test result."

The verdict was clear – Aarya had Niemann Pick Type C. It was the dangerous and incurable type. And it was due to genetic factors.

Shital felt like the walls were closing in. What could one do after such a diagnosis? It was virtually a death sentence.

"We visited everyone. Nobody knew what to do."

Niemann Pick C was a rare disease. Only a handful of cases have been reported in India. And most doctors had very limited knowledge of its treatment.

With the lack of information, Shital grew more desperate. Her baby was counting on her – she had to do something.

So she started looking elsewhere for help. From homeopathy to flower therapy, she tried everything.

"We went a homeopathy doctor in Ratnagiri. His medicines we tried. *But kuch nahi hua.* So we stopped."

Eventually, she realised that things were only getting worse. By the time Aarya turned three, the first signs of deterioration were visible.

"It started with eating. He kept coughing and didn't want to swallow."

Shital's heart broke every time she saw her son struggling to swallow. She thought to herself that if she could find parents of Niemann Pick C patients, surely they would know how to help Aarya. So she spent hours searching on the Internet. But only one website was helpful.

'Hope For Aaditya' was a site started by the family of

a Niemann Pick C patient. When Shital contacted the parents they were extremely kind and helpful. At last, she had found someone who could understand 'what I am going through'.

"The Dasguptas also showed me how to take care of Aarya on a day-to-day basis."

They explained to Shital that her son would need a peg in order to eat. This peg would prevent food from entering the lungs. But to insert the peg, Aarya would need an endoscopic gastrostomy. The little boy was only three years old when he bravely underwent this difficult surgery.

For every little complication, Shital looked to the Dasguptas for advice.

"They told us how much worse it was going to get. How much my Aarya would suffer. But without them, I could have done nothing for him. Whatever little I did, that also I wouldn't have been able to do."

It was more help than any of the doctors had given her. But it was not enough. "These were things to make Aarya comfortable. Not cure him."

And a mother fighting for her son was not about to

give up so easily.

As the months passed, Aarya was gradually slipping away from her. He had lost the ability to crawl, to talk, to cry out 'Mumma' when he needed her.

"And then I heard of a new drug. It could arrest further deterioration, not cure it. But this was enough. At least I wouldn't lose my Aarya."

In 2011, this drug cost almost ₹5 lakhs for a batch of 90 tablets. And every three months a new batch of tablets had to be bought.

Shital and Vikrant knew the financial pressure this medicine would put on them. But there was no option – anything to save Aarya.

When she asked one of her doctors if there was any chance of getting a discount, the insensitivity of the reply hurt her deeply.

"Your request is as absurd as asking for a Mercedes at a discount."

"It was not a luxury I was asking a discount for. It was a life-saving drug for my son. Does he not have a right to live?"

Shital's troubles did not stop there. Since the

medicines were imported, clearing customs became a major hurdle. No doctors or hospitals came to her aid, and managing the red tape became her headache.

It took over a month-and-a-half for the medicines to clear customs. All that precious time that she could have spent with her son, wasted on paperwork.

As Aarya started taking the medicines, hope bloomed in Shital's heart. But in a few months, Shital realised the drugs were not working.

"I plunged into despair, *karoon toh kya karoon...*"

Through all this, Shital's sister Rachna was her rock, explaining complicated medical stuff because she was a PhD in Pharmaceuticals. She even moved from Bengaluru to Mumbai to be with her sister.

In the struggle to care for Aarya, Shital realised that people just did not know about his disease. There was an urgent need to create awareness. So she started distributing pamphlets in Mumbai's hospitals.

"I knew there must be parents like us, desperate for information."

She also began a trust called 'With Aarya' that would focus on the Niemann Pick disorder.

"I suffered terrible isolation and loneliness. If there is someone like me in your circle with a very sick child – give them your support. It makes a big difference."

"We were educated and had access to the Internet. That is why we were able to know at least something about this horrible disease. Imagine the condition of poor people who can't even afford the diagnosis. What would happen to them?"

Through the trust, Shital advocated clinical trials for new drugs and even reached out to the government to get concessions on existing drugs. As a mother, she did everything she could. Her main aim was to tell as many people as she could about Niemann Pick. For if enough people knew, maybe things would change....

These initiatives were usually met with a lot of resistance. The government was focused on more widespread diseases like AIDS and cancer. The standard answer she got was, "*Madam bachche bhookhe mar rahe hain, agar unhein dene ke liye paise nahin hai*, how are we going to sponsor expensive medicines?"

Hurt by their callous attitude, Shital turned her attention to helping parents take care of children with similar problems. Lending a patient ear to them and giving them all the information she wished she had got when Aarya was younger.

As time passed, Shital began noticing that Aarya's health was still deteriorating, slowly but surely.

"He wasn't moving his right arm anymore. He kept it curled to his chest." His eyes had also lost their twinkle.

Every time he had a fever, Shital worried that it was time. And each time he returned from hospital, she knew that he was slipping away.

Her husband Vikrant was by her side, grieving quietly. He could see the bubbly girl he'd married sliding into depression. So he encouraged her to find something to do, to divert her mind.

After a lot of coaxing, Shital decided to open a beauty salon near her home in Sewri, Mumbai. It helped relieve some of her stress, to go out of the house, talk to new people. It almost made her feel normal.

The last few months with Aarya were heart-breaking for Shital. She watched him disappear every day, till one day, three months before his seventh birthday, he passed away peacefully.

"We knew it was coming but still … I felt a huge void, an emptiness."

For seven long years, Aarya had been Shital's whole and sole focus. Her purpose of existing. A new phase of life was calling her now – but was Shital ready for it?

There are people who are swept away in the river of sorrow. And there are those who somehow find the strength to swim to the shore. Shital found that strength.

"I can never forget Aarya … he is always in my heart. But I know he would want his mumma to be happy. So I must try to be happy."

Shital began taking more interest in her salon. As soon as her daughter left for school, she would go to the parlour and supervise the staff, manage the accounts.

Business at the salon improved by leaps and bounds. Within a few months, Shital had expanded the salon by renting a neighbouring shop.

But the work that continues to be the most fulfilling

is helping parents of Niemann Pick-afflicted children. These interactions often bring back a flood of memories, but Shital knows she must do what she can – to help those in need.

Shital is also a volunteer with Make-A-Wish India – a foundation dedicated to making the last wish of a terminally-ill child come true. She spends two days a week working with this foundation.

The work involves visiting hospitals and interacting with families of young patients. Explaining how the child can make a wish. Shital also assists with the paperwork and follows up till the wish is fulfilled.

"When a child's face lights up I see Aarya smiling down at me. I *feel* his presence..."

Her latest initiative is arranging food packets for families of patients – dal-khichdi, roti-sabzi and a fruit (banana). The meals are distributed outside Tata Memorial, KEM and Wadia hospitals for a subsidised price of ₹10. Volunteers and donations from wellswishers make this possible (http://www.withaarya.ngo for details).

"Don Ghaas (which means meal in Marathi) is my way of helping families going through the same turmoil that I did…" says the mother whose son is no more.

For a mother's heart is big and strong and overflowing with love. And love never dies, love is eternal.

Besharam

"Hai, thodi toh sharam kar" – ladkiyon ko dabaa ke rakhne ka ek acchha tareeka. Is liye besharam bano, ooncha socho, aage badho…. Log yun hi sharam jayenge.*

*(There is no good English word for the term 'sharm' or 'besharam') 'Be modest' – this is what girls are told so they stay where they are. So be bold, think big, move ahead…. Others will follow.

Saatvi Paas Sarpanch

Sushma Bhadu
Dhani Miyan Khan, Haryana

"Aurat ko dabaa ke rakho – keep her behind a veil."
But do women want to stay hidden under the ghunghat?
When Sushma Bhadu became sarpanch she seized the moment and challenged the tradition.

"Tanney sunnya kay!" boomed a Haryanvi matron through her pink ghunghat. *"Hamaare gaon mein Panchayat baithegi!"*

Sushma Bhadu was patiently waiting in queue along with the women from her village – Dhani Miyan Khan – for the *pani ka* tanker. That January evening there was a leher of excitement. The conversation was not about the usual *ghar ki* problems and *saas ki kit-kit.* Even the preparations for the upcoming Lohri festival had taken a backseat.

Since Independence, Dhani Miyan Khan and its two adjoining villages had been under the *chhatra-chhaya* of the district collector of Fatehabad town. The residents never had a say in any matter related to their own welfare. Now, in 2010, the state government had decided that Dhani Miyan Khan could elect its own Panchayat.

But there was a small catch. In fact it was a very BIG catch. The position of Sarpanch was reserved for a woman.

"Hai rabba, sarkaar da dimaag kharaab hoyya si!" muttered the menfolk. How could they put such a

strange and unreasonable condition? Surely no woman would come forward ... and ultimately the post would go to a deserving mard.

But the women had other plans. *Pehli baar ek mauka mila tha, uska fayda uthaana zaroori tha.* That evening, as they waited for the water tanker, they hatched a plan.

"Sushma – tu saat tak padhi hui hai. Tu hi hamaari taraf se khadi ho...!" they pleaded.

Sushma was taken aback. She had never thought of herself as a 'leader'. Yes, she had studied till 7th standard, but like all the other women in Dhani Miyan Khan, her life was in the *chaar-diwaari* of her home. What did she know about becoming a Sarpanch?

The women coaxed her, cajoled her. *Aadmiyon ko kya pata auraton ke sar ke bojh.*

"Raat ko hum nau nau baje tak pani ke liye tanki ke pass hi baithe rehte hain. Tu Sarpanch banegi toh hamari yeh samasya toh mit jaawe!"

The women in Dhani Miyan Khan decided to put complete faith in one of their own. You stand, we will support you, they assured Sushma.

"Thaare khilaaf aur koi nahin khada hoga," they

decided. And what a wise decision it was.

The other two villages fielded more than two candidates each. They were the wives of influential men. On election day, votes were split among these multiple *ummeedwaars*, but in Dhani Miyan Khan, there was just one candidate, one vote.

Sushma Bhadu was declared the new Sarpanch. It was the first time in 63 years that a woman had stepped out of her traditional role. Into the *baahar ki duniya* dominated by men.

But becoming the Sarpanch was one thing, being *accepted* was quite another. Many had thought that Sushma would be a *naam ke vastey* leader. That they would be able to control her and get her to do their bidding.

"Mahila thi toh logon ko dikkat thi. Yeh karo woh karo kehte rehte the..."

For two years Sushma tried working within the strict confines of *reeti-riwaaz*. One of the main hurdles was the *ghunghat* she was expected to cover her face with – at all times.

"Maine kaha ji Sarpanch toh aapne bana diya par yeh ghunghat odh ke main kaam kaise karoon?"

How do I talk to people who come with their problems? How do I go to the district administration to solve these problems? All the time, Sushma felt hampered. The *ghunghat* was restricting her, constricting her.

Sushma recalled an earlier time in her life, when she was a *nayi dulhan*. It had been a shock to enter a home where she had to cover her face and wear the traditional lehenga kameez.

"Yeh jo hamare husband the, wo mujhe dhakke se lehenga kameez pehnate they. Mujhe bahut dikkat hoti thi aise. Wo kahe yeh pehle ka riwaaz he, yeh toh pehenna hi padega."

In her parents' home, Sushma had been relatively free. *Chaar bhaiyon mein akeli behen, sabki laadli.* Besides, her father was forward-thinking. He had sent Sushma to school till 7th standard, when most other girls dropped out by 4th standard.

It was probably this upbringing that had given Sushma the courage to stand up to her husband after her daughter was born.

"Ya toh mujhse yeh baccha sambhala jayega ya lehenga kameez pehna jayega!" she declared.

Faced with such an ultimatum, her husband meekly agreed and Sushma started wearing Punjabi suits. That had been a small, hard-earned victory, and now she decided it was time to do something bigger.

"Apni behnon ke liye kuch karna hoga, ladna hoga … main taiyaar thi!"

The women in the village work mostly in the fields. Picking cotton with a ghunghat covering the face is difficult, more so in the scorching summer season. In fact, they cannot even clearly see what they are picking. So the cotton they pick is 'unclean' and, hence, women are paid less than men.

"Aagey badhna hai toh yeh ghunghat pratha hataani hogi … humne toh yeh thaan li."

It was time for the Sarpanch to assert herself. But Sushma knew that change must begin at home. First, she would have to convince her own family.

"Maine kaha, Sarpanch ke kaam mein ghunghat se bahut dikkat hai. Main yeh pratha khatam chahti hoon."

The family was shocked to hear this. But then her mother-in-law came forward in support.

"Tu sahi bol rahi hai, bahu. Main tere saath hoon."

With *sasuma* by her side, Sushma declared to the village that she was removing her ghunghat. Then she encouraged others to join her. There was tremendous resistance from the *bade-buzurg* of the village. So Sushma decided to pass a formal resolution.

"Humne pehle chhoti si panchayat baithayi. Anganwadi worker, aise hi do teen member bula ke. Phir wo bole hum bhi sehmat hai is baat se."

This victory gave her immense confidence, and she decided to share her message on a much larger platform. *"Phir humne mahapanchayat baithayi thi ek. Kam se kam pachees chabbis gaon ki panchayat thi."*

Mahapanchayats are usually rare events. In Fatehabad, Mahapanchayats were convened only when there was a drought or flood situation, or when the state elections were due.

Having called for this Mahapanchayat, it was up to Sushma to rally the audience. Even the local media was present to cover the event.

Sushma could feel the eyes of the crowd boring into her. Normally, she would have hidden behind a *ghunghat* in front of so many people. But that day, neither she nor her *sahyogis* had a veil to hide behind.

Even as Sarpanch, Sushma had never addressed such a large gathering. But this was a 'moment of truth'. She *had* to give it her best.

"Maine Anganwadi mahilaon ki taraf dekha.... Unka sahyog nahin hota toh shayad bol nahin paati."

Sushma took a deep breath and began her speech. There was nothing written down, or pre-planned.

"Par jaise hum bolne lage, bas bolte gaye. Phir nahi rukna tha..."

Her voice was loud, confident. Her thoughts were clear and appealing. By the time she finished, Sushma had won over her audience. They joined her in taking an oath.

"Hum sab ne shapath li ki hum ghungat pratha nahi karenge. Sabhi mahilaon ne mere saath diya."

The local newspapers gave this gutsy Sarpanch front-page coverage. Soon the national media was knocking on her door. With articles and television news channels lauding this as a radical step towards modernity, the villagers found it easier to accept this change.

"Akhbaar mein aaya, TV mein aaya, toh bhai sab

acchha bole. Gaon ke log sunkar padhkar bole ki sahi mein acchha hua."

Though a few did grumble about women becoming besharam, it was difficult for her opponents to do anything publicly.

Since that momentous day in June 2012, the village of Dhani Miyan Khan is almost completely *ghunghat*-free. You still see women with their faces covered, but it is only to protect their skin from the sun. The eyes are free to see the open sky, the green fields. And of course, the delicate cotton buds.

"Ab khet mein koi paresaani na howe…"

The women's wages are now almost at par with the men's.

With one small act of defiance, Sushma Bhadu became Sarpanch of her village not just in name, but in thought, word and deed. She has worked tirelessly for the greater good of all.

With the help of the district collector, Sushma got borewells dug in the village. No more *paani ki killat,* no more waiting for tankers. The role of Sarpanch, she says, is to take the needs of the people to the administration.

And then, to get the job done.

"Sarkaar paise deti hai, humein uska sahi upyog karna hai."

With Sushma at the helm, there is not a single allegation of corruption. *Chaaron taraf* development is visible. Yet, at times people oppose the Sarpanch in her work.

"Jab nayi sadak ban rahi thi kuch logon ne kaha hum nahin banne denge. Baat police thane tak pahunch gayi."

The issue was resolved when Collector sahib came, inspected the area and declared the plans to be correct. *Sadak yaheen banegi.* Today, nearly all the *kuccha* roads have been made *pakka*, and they are are well connected to the highways. There is no *keechad*, no *gandgi*.

Sushma's mother-in-law adds, with obvious pride, *"Iske aane se kaafi sudhaar ho gaya hai yahaan. Hamari sadak ab Chandigarh jaisi hai!"*

These are the visible changes, but Sushma is also working at a deeper level. She believes that education for girls is the real solution to most problems.

"Hamaare jamaane mein ladkiyon ko sheeksha nahin mili. Ab toh bahut value hai padhaai ki, unhe zaroor milni chahiye."

"Aagey badhne ke liye humein aagey kadam uthhaana padhega."

Thus, Sushma is working towards improving the teaching standards in government schools. She has also mobilised government funds to give free books to all students. For girls, there is a special endowment of ₹11,000 and a washing machine if they are married after the legal age of 18 years. All these measures have made her a very popular Sarpanch and brought her closer to the people.

In all these efforts, she has faced serious opposition. But to the virodhis, she offers a simple logic: *"Gaon aage badhega bhai toh gaon ka hi naam roshan hoga. Gaon aagey badhega toh tu bhi bhai aagey badhega."*

Perhaps the biggest hurdle in her path had been her own husband. But now he is a strong support, an advocate of women's empowerment, and represents the village in forums where he speaks against the *ghunghat pratha*.

"Abhi inke sahyog se kaafi kaam ho jave hai," says Sushma.

For her efforts, Sushma has received several awards and felicitations. But the one closest to her heart is the Jijabhai Women Achievers' Award given to her by Shivaji College, New Delhi. It is not the award itself that means so much to her, but the pride she felt when she addressed the students.

"Wahan toh sab Angrezi bolne waale bacche the. Par main boli, hum toh bhai apni bhaasa mein bolenge."

The English-medium students were bowled over by Sushma's *bolne ka lehja* and more so by the content of her speech, straight from the heart.

After so many achievements, Sushma is not one to relax. Today, there is a sense of urgency, for her term is almost over. And there is so much more to be done!

Despite her good work, Sushma cannot be re-elected. The seat has been reserved for a Scheduled Caste candidate. But she is happy to support the next Sarpanch, to continue the good work.

"Poora sahyog hum karenge unka."

They say that change takes time, but the times are changing. *Ek aurat ki soch se ek gaon ki soch badal gayi.*

Toh socho, agar har aurat ki soch badal jaaye toh yeh desh badal sakta hai.

Now *that* would really be something!

Chak de Periods!

Aditi Gupta
Ahmedabad, Gujarat

"Don't enter the temple – you are unclean." This is what Indian girls are told by their mothers and grandmothers. But why? Why should a girl be made to feel 'abnormal' about this natural process? Yehi sach jaanne ke liye Aditi Gupta ne halla bola. Zor se, aur apni style mein.

"Do you bleed this much every month?" Tuhin Paul asked his girlfriend Aditi Gupta.

He knew about something called a 'period', but exactly how it affected a girl – that he was seeing for the first time. For that one week of the month Aditi was not her usual self. She was sad, irritable and often had stomach cramps.

Aditi was touched by Tuhin's concern for her. So she told him all that she knew about it: it happens every month, to every girl. And in 'those days', girls are 'ashudh'.

In the small town of Garhwa in Jharkhand where Aditi grew up, the M word was never uttered. It was all hush-hush and top secret.

Older cousins used code language to explain why they could not visit the temple on 'those' days. *Jaise ki "Aaj baal nahin dhoye hain"*. Every one would quietly understand what it meant.

Aditi was in 7th standard when she first got her 'monthly'. It was only after she started bleeding that her mother explained – there is something called a 'period'. It is messy, painful and women must suffer in silence.

"Mummy ne mujhe dhaai lote paani se nahlaaya. Bole

ki dhaai lota paani hai toh period dhaai din rahega."

Of course, it did not work! *Yun toh* mummy was a professor in the university – highly educated – but she offered no explanation. And thus began Aditi's monthly cycle of shame and discomfort.

Sanitary napkins were not so common back then. Most girls used a soft cotton cloth. This created two big problems: firstly, cycling to school with a cloth between your legs (it was painful!); and secondly, how to wash and where to dry such that no one would see it.

Even the clothes Aditi wore during her periods had to be washed separately. Because that was the 'rule'. And these rules were endless.

Baal dhona padega.

Bedsheet bhi.

Achaar mat chhoona.

Bhagwanji ko mat chhoona.

Khhatta kam khao – khhatta khaane se periods badh jaate hain.

Do this, don't do this – how stressful and irritating all these rules were!

School was no better. Most girls got their period in 7th standard, but the chapter on reproduction appeared only in 9th standard. There were two parts: one about how cells multiply, the other about how humans multiply.

"Teacher ne pehla chapter padhaya, par doosra skip kar diya!"

Even if you dared to peek into the textbook all you would see were scientific diagrams. There was no practical information: about hygiene or cramps or what to do if your period started in school.

Only one point was clear – this is a taboo subject.

Aditi saw advertisements for sanitary napkins on TV but how could she go out and buy such an item? *Sab ko pata chal jayega, na!*

It was only when she went to live in a hostel in 11th and 12th in Ranchi that Aditi made friends with girls who regularly used napkins. And talked about it. She gathered the courage to go to a chemist and whisper to the shopkeeper, *"Mujhe pads chahiye."*

The shopkeeper discreetly wrapped the pads in a black polythene bag and gave it to her.

Switching from cloth to napkins made Aditi feel light and free. Free from shame and that feeling of dirtiness when she was in 'that time of the month'.

And now, Tuhin wanted to know: "Why do you bleed?"

But what was the 'right' answer to give him?

That's when Tuhin and Aditi decided – we will look for these answers together.

First they began reading up material on the Internet. As they continued their research, Aditi and Tuhin realised how ill-informed they were.

"I didn't even know the composition of my menstrual fluid. I thought I was losing a lot of blood, when most of it is only mucus."

Aditi and Tuhin were boyfriend-girlfriend, and they were also classmates. Both were pursuing a postgraduate course in Visual Communication at NID (National Institute of Design, Ahmedabad). And they often worked together on projects.

Now, the final diploma project was coming up and they needed to find an interesting topic to work on. It was Tuhin who insisted – let's take up menstruation and the myths surrounding it.

Aditi liked the idea. With Tuhin by her side, she began talking to her friends on campus. Soon she found out that even the open-minded NID students were also shy about talking about periods.

If that was the situation in NID, imagine what was happening in small towns. Something had to be done.

Over the next one year Aditi visited schools, colleges and NGOs to understand what exactly was the mindset of people. This was not as easy as one would think, since teachers refused to cooperate.

"Many teachers think if they talk about sex in class, students will start having sex. They destroy educational material, saying that *bachche corrupt ho jayenge.*"

It took a lot of effort, but when students started opening up, their stories came tumbling out. Whether it was an elite school in Ahmedabad or a government school in Mehsana, the girls had little or no proper information.

"Lekin har jagah yeh tha ki periods ke time kuch galat ho raha hai, kuch ganda ho raha hai."

And this was surely affecting a young girl's self-esteem, her psyche.

Aditi conducted some of the research in her own hometown. This wasn't easy, especially because she included her 13-year-old brother as a part of the study.

People did what they do best – started gossiping

"Har jagah yeh tha ki periods ke time kuch galat ho raha hai, kuch ganda ho raha hai."

about what Aditi was doing.

"Everyone felt I should get a stable job and not waste my time like this!"

But Aditi and Tuhin did not get disturbed. It is never easy to change minds. This they knew from the very start. Now, the challenge before them was *how* to spread awareness. What kind of communication would work?

"Since we are both engineers and Tuhin is very good with animation, we first thought of creating a computer game."

But not every girl would have easy access to a computer.

"How about a comic book!" said Tuhin.

Tuhin had read that comic books were an effective way to talk about taboo subjects like domestic violence. It was the perfect medium to address girls between 9 and 14.

"We had collected a lot of stories from all over

India. Every community had its own myths around menstruation!"

Aditi and Tuhin decided to use these stories, along with practical information, to prepare a young girl for her first period. They created an A3-size Hindi comic book with three characters who had various doubts and questions. These were answered by a young doctor *didi* called Priya.

"Hamein bahut care se comic banani padi. Like we did not use any objectionable images."

A girl had to be able to read it with her parents without feeling embarassed.

A prototype of the comic was tested with 400 schoolgirls and received an enthusiastic response. But college was coming to an end and the couple had no money to pursue this any further. So both Aditi and Tuhin took up jobs. Then they got married.

But they could never get their project out of their minds. So they decided to start a blog, which was very well received. This gave them confidence and, in August 2012, both quit their jobs.

"We decided to first launch a website called *Menstrupedia*."

This would contain all the information a girl needed to have about her period, and a forum where girls can ask questions.

"We put our own savings into building the website. On the technology side, we had the help of our friend Rajat Mittal, who is a Master's in Computer Science."

They also wanted a doctor on board who could review the information on the website. They approached many doctors but none had the time or interest to be an advisor.

Despite such hurdles, the *Menstrupedia* website went live on 29 October 2012. In the beginning they did not get many visitors, but slowly the number of visitors increased. The media also extensively covered them. Parents and teachers and young girls themselves sent a lot of positive feedback.

A gynaecologist based in the UK got in touch to say 'I want to help'. So answering the questions became his job.

Many visitors asked, "Can we buy the comic book?"

But printing a book required a lot of money, and by March 2013, the couple had exhausted their savings. Nor could they find an investor.

Then Tuhin and Aditi came up with a brilliant plan. What if we make the *'aam admi'* our angel investor? This is called 'crowdfunding', i.e. many people contribute small sums if they like your idea and want to make it a reality.

Aditi and Tuhin listed their project on a crowdfunding website called Wishberry. Their aim was to raise ₹4 lakh to print 1,000 copies of the comic. Initially they were nervous – would anyone come forward to invest? In less than an hour, the first ₹1,000 had come in.

"When the campaign ended, we had raised more than ₹5 lakh from 175 generous donors across 85 cities. *Ek bahut bada boost mila hamein!*"

In January 2014, 1,000 copies of the *Menstrupedia* comic book in English were ready for distribution... With the book in hand, Aditi started doing workshops in schools.

"Jidhar bhi workshop kiya there was a lot of interest, a lot of questions."

Today, *Menstrupedia* is available in Hindi, Marathi, Gujarati and Kannada. More than 8,000 books have been sold and 4,000 copies distributed free of cost to schools. The website, too, gets more than 1 lakh visitors a month.

Aditi and Tuhin know the road ahead is long. The plan is to translate the book in all regional languages and set up an online store for menstrual products. Even launch an app.

Now Aditi's family is also very happy about what *beti* and *damaad* are doing. When she appeared on NDTV to debate the 'Happy to Bleed' campaign, both her mother and father were very proud.

But the most beautiful part is the support of Tuhin. *Agar ek ladka aur ladki haath mein haath ek doosre ke saath sangharsh karein toh kya kuch nahin badal sakta.* Because all that is needed is one generation to change this mindset. *Aur yeh problem khud hi solve ho jayegi.*

Suniye Sisterji

Hafiza Khan
Srinagar, Kashmir

"Ladkiyon ko hum iskool nahin bhejte." This mindset prevails all over the country, Srinagar is no exception. Hafiza Khan ko yeh manzoor na tha. She worked tirelessly for 25 years to get an education for every girl in her mohalla. All are now grateful for the efforts of 'Sisterji'.

"Meri ma ne ma ka pyaar bhi diya aur baap ka pyaar bhi."

Hafiza was born in Kishtwar in Jammu district, the third among four sisters. Her father disappeared when she was very young. Perhaps he went away because one more daughter was born to him — nobody knows, but he was never seen again.

When Hafiza was five years old, the family shifted to Srinagar. They lived in a small rented house.

"Ma ghar-ghar mein bartan dhoti thi ... paisa kama kar laati thi, aise hamein bada kiya."

Like all little girls, Hafiza loved to play with her sisters and friends. But she was also fascinated by the *iskool* right opposite her house. She would stand there for hours, watching the children in school uniform, listening to the lessons going on.

Hafiza's mother could not afford to give her daughters an education. Luckily, they found out about a government social welfare home in the Shalimar area of Srinagar which provided free education. All four sisters enrolled there.

The school was Urdu medium till 8th standard; in 9th standard, all subjects were taught in English.

"Mujhe English theek se aati nahi thi toh phir maine

8th ke baad school chhod diya."

Hafiza then started doing various kinds of odd jobs. Some papier mâché work, some handicrafts. But she would never stick to any one thing. Her mother, Mehar Bano, once joked, *"Hafiza tu har mahine kaam badalti hai, kya husband bhi badlegi?"*

Mehar Bano had a very free and frank relationship with her daughters.

"Maa hamari saheli thi ... agar kabhi hamein koi ladka chhedta tha toh hum jaakar maa ko bolte the. Hum ne kabhi bhi ma se koi baat chhupai nahi."

When Hafiza fell in love with Mohammed she did not hesitate to tell her mother. Ammi was happy that her daughter had found a life-partner and gave her blessings. Thus, at the age of 21, Hafiza embarked on a new life. A very different life from what she had led so far.

"Mere husband anpadh the ... sab log mujhse puchte the kya kar rahi hai. Kya wahan adjust ho payegi? Par shaadi toh dil ki baat hai."

Hafiza's *sasuraal* was in an area of Srinagar known as Dal Gate. It is connected to the city only through a narrow dirt path with the lake on both sides. During the rainy season and in winter, the residents were practically cut off. Hence Dal Gate remained backward, almost like a village.

Her husband's family was large – one married brother and three unmarried sisters – all under one roof. There were many mouths to feed and never enough money. Hafiza was not one to sit idle. She began doing *aari* (hand embroidery) work to bring in some money.

She even taught her sister-in-law and other girls in the village the same craft.

But the work Hafiza really enjoyed was teaching. In the evenings, she would round up the teenage boys in the neighbourhood and tutor them.

"Wo ladke kehte the ki aap bahut achchi tarah samjhaate ho. Toh mujhe achcha laga."

The classes were held in the evening and often there would be a power cut. Any other woman might have got scared – *ki itne mard aur main akeli aurat.* But Hafiza had complete faith that nothing wrong would happen.

"Mujhe ek alag bharosa tha apne aap par…"

In Want mohalla, there was also a government centre providing NFE (Non-Formal Education) classes. When the centre head realised that Hafiza was '8th standard pass' he offered her a part-time job.

"Main us mohalle ki akeli padhi-likhi aurat thi. Is liye bina experience ke main teacher ban gayi."

For one hour every day, Hafiza held an informal class for young girls where she taught them how to sign their name, do a little addition-subtraction, read some Urdu.

"Zyada toh kuch nahi sirf sau rupaye milte the ... par yeh kaam mera kudrati shauk hai!"

Hafiza managed to teach 60–70 girls through the NFE classes. While the girls were eager to learn more and even go to school, their parents were hardly bothered.

This, she could see in her own family. One of Hafiza's *nanads* passed away, leaving behind five young daughters. Her dying wish was that Hafiza should raise her daughters.

"Main apne bete ke saath uski badi beti ko iskool bhejna chahti thi par uska baap raazi na tha."

There was a lot of *shor-sharaaba*. Why are you sticking your neck out for that child, people asked. Mind your own business, they said. But Hafiza was determined. In fact, what she did was cleverly enrol the girl in a school run by Sheikh Abdullah's wife. She did this knowing that the girl's father would not have the guts to face the begum.

"Aaj wahi ladki 9th pass hai aur apne baap ka sahara hai."

This urge to help the weak, the underdog, was always in Hafiza. Even if she saw someone beating up a dog on the street she would rush to the rescue.

"Mujhe bardasht nahi hota tha … ma kehti thi ki ek din tu apne aap ko fasaa legi."

These kinds of warnings never stopped Hafiza from doing what she thought was right.

She would visit the homes of girls in her mohalla and counsel the parents. You are educating your boys? Very good. But you must educate the girls also. Why? It is for your own benefit.

And slowly, very slowly, they accepted this idea. One day, an invitation card arrived at someone's house. And a girl, who had been attending NFE classes, was able to read the name of the sender. Her father was overjoyed.

He came up to Hafiza and said, *"Sisterji aaj hamari izzat bach gayi."*

'Sisterji' became the name by which Hafiza became known in Want mohalla. A mark of respect, a mark of affection.

But despite all these efforts, very few children went to a proper school. The closest school was an hour away and had only one teacher. *Wo bhi kabhi aata tha, kabhi nahin.*

In 1999, an NGO called Secure Future came to Want mohalla.

"Unhone yahan par private school khola aur bachchon ko padhana shuru kiya."

The NGO recruited two boys who were 12th pass and Hafiza who was 8th pass. The boys never came to work sincerely so it was Hafiza who became the project coordinator.

But getting students was not easy. They were all busy helping their parents. Some were fishing, some were farming, some were weaving straw mats. *Hamein school jaane ka kya fayda?* Hafiza's job was to change this mindset.

Lekin itna badi baat shuru kaise karein? By first changing something very basic.

The first thing Hafiza started was a *safaai abhiyaan.* To teach kids about hygiene and cleanliness.

"Bachchon ke nakhun bade hote the, unmein mail hota tha, aangan gande hua karte the … humne is par pehle kaam shuru kiya."

She involved the kids by teaching them a song about cleanliness — *'Mujhe saaf karo'*.

Bimariya bhi kuch kam nahi, phir bhi tumko kuch gam nahi.

Mahaul pe apne insaaf karo, mujhe saaf karo, mujhe saaf karo.

At first, they learnt to keep their classroom clean. Then, twice a week, they would pick up a *jhaadu* and do *safaai* of the entire mohalla.

"Log hairaan the ki yeh kya ho raha hai ... par phir unko achcha laga. Dil khush hua."

Then, to attract more children to the school, Hafiza used a novel method. She would stand at the street corner with a *dhol*. A crowd would quickly gather, and then she would sing songs and tell stories. To motivate them — *aap bhi iskool aaiye*.

To attract girls, Hafiza would call them to class and play games like carrom. They would also sing songs and tell jokes to each other. Then, one day, without anyone noticing, Sisterji would introduce the concept of mathematics. *Hisaab kitna jaroori hai*. She would teach addition and subtraction using things from everyday life.

"Wo log roz saag baandhte the toh usme tinka hota hai,

usse ginti sikhaana shuru kiya."

Slowly, the girls started enjoying these classes. They would hurry up and finish their housework so they could come to school.

There were mixed reactions to these new developments. A few people supported Hafiza, but many were unhappy.

"Kuch logon ne meri badnaami shuru kar di … ki iske baap ka koi pata nahin hai."

Hafiza swallowed these bitter insults. She was brave and calm in public.

"Main roti thi … magar chupke chupke."

The worst was yet to come. One morning she found that someone had printed an insulting poster and stuck it on the wall of her house. *Bura toh laga*, but instead of breaking down, Hafiza expressed her emotions creatively. She began writing small *shayaris*.

Zindabaad zindabaad. Secure Future NGO zindabaad.

Mere liye Kamal Kashmir banaya, NFE class isme chalaya.

Mera dil hua shaad, zindabaad zindabaad.

Jo khushi dena tha apno ne meri,

Wo khushi mili SF ke dere,

Zindagi hui aabaad, zindabaad.
Moti maala me khushiya hai aayi,
Bachcho ne milkar kasam hai khayi.
Honge hum kamyaab, zindabaaad zindabaad.

No doubt Hafiza could fight against the outsiders who opposed her work. But the real test of her courage was yet to come.

When people realised that Hafiza would not give in, they tried to influence her husband. They whispered all kinds of things in his ears until, finally, he got brainwashed and flew off the handle.

"Tujhe agar yahi kaam karna hai ti main tujhe talaq de dunga!" he shouted.

Hafiza took a tough stand. She said, *"Kamaal hai is waqt aapko mera saath dena chahiye na ki mohallewalonka!"*

All I am doing is educating girls. This is not against morality. This is not against the law.

"Phir bhi agar tum talaaq dena chahte ho toh yeh bhi yaad rakhna main yahan se nikalne waali nahin hoon."

Sisterji would stay in the same mohalla and continue her work. Until each and every child started going to school.

"Agar ladki kamau hogi, padhi likhi hogi toh sasural bhi chala sakti hai aur ma-baap ka bhi khayal rakh sakti hai."

Hafiza's husband relented. Okay – you do your work, I will not stop you! And Sisterji has never looked back since.

Hafiza's work extended beyond children, to the mothers. She would hold classes to teach them small-small things like *waqt ki pabandi* – the importance of being on time.

More and more families in Want mohalla understood the value of education. With help from Hafiza, they were able to enrol in the government school. Today, more than 20 of these children are college graduates.

"Shuru mein gaaliya di lekin is time Sisterji kehte hue thakte nahi hai…" she laughs.

Sisterji settles family disputes, counsels husbands and wives, sometimes simply lends a listening ear. If you tell Sisterji something, it remains with Sisterji. That you can trust!

Over the years, Hafiza has created awareness for immunisation. And the need to register births and deaths. She has trained girls to do embroidery work so they can earn and be self-sufficient.

"Aaj har ek aurat ke paas paise hai. Bank mein apna account hai!"

And the girls are much smarter, they don't get fooled by Romeo-type boys. They are confident, they know their mind. If a girl really likes a boy who is deserving of her affections, she goes up to her parents and says, *"Hum shaadi karna chahte hain."*

"Usme kya galat hai," says Hafiza.

Hafiza's own children – three sons and a daughter – are now grown up and very proud of their mother. Her husband is most cooperative. He knows that even on Sunday Hafiza cannot sit at home and relax. *Kahin na kahin se uske liye bulawa aa jayega!*

How did she manage when the children were young? That's where the joint family system came to her rescue.

"Mere devar aur nanad ne bachchon ko paala – mujh par koi tension nahi tha!"

Tension is one thing that Hafiza has learned to eliminate from her life. She believes that *'aman'* or peace has to begin from the home. And it is women who have to show the way forward. By keeping a check on their sharp tongues.

"Jab koi bhi ladai karta hai, hamari auratein jawab nahi diya karti. Wo kehti ki isse kya hoga, ladai karne se!"

Many family disputes and *roz ke jhagde* have been solved by this unusual approach.

Hafiza believes that men and women were created equal by God. But they have different strengths.

"Kudrat ne mardon ko jismaani taakat di hai aur auratonko ko ruhaani taakat di hai."

For a girl may be physically weaker, but she is mentally stronger. Strong enough to take charge of herself, her family and the entire world.

Band-Aid Family

Swati Karwa
Nagpur, Maharashtra

"You are married – you must tolerate everything for your family." When cracks appeared in Swati's marriage, she had two choices: stay and suffer in silence, or leave with her dignity intact. She chose to leave. And build a new life for herself.

Swati Karwa could not remember how long she had been sitting alone in the darkness. But she couldn't gather the strength to get up.

An hour ago, she had asked her husband a question: *Kya aap ka affair chal raha?* Somewhere in her heart, she already knew the answer, but she still needed him to say it.

He confessed. He was having an affair.

Swati Karwa had spent 15 years of her life building a home and family. "I was born here in Nagpur, and I had a very peaceful childhood, no major issues. *Dukh toh kabhi dekhe hi nahi.* And, I fell in love with Sunil, when I was in the 11th standard, 12th something. After seven years of courtship, we got married."

The young couple knew that the first few years would be tough, but they thought love could conquer all. Sunil was just starting out in his business and had zero income, while Swati was busy trying to be the perfect *bahu* for her new family.

He was in Pune and she was in Kamlapur. But they nurtured the hope that, one day, things would turn around. They had so much to be thankful for – how many couples get their parents' permission for a love marriage?

"Mujhe aise feeling tha ki maine uske family ko bahut takleef di hai. Yeh shaadi accept kiya hai. Jitna bhi wo kar sakte hai, they are doing it. *Toh*, it is my duty now to make them happy."

In the first year of marriage, Swati and her husband hardly met each other. So, when she finally got an opportunity to shift to Pune, she was excited. She was four months pregnant then.

"Chhota sa ghar tha, usko set kiya. It was a very good feeling. We didn't have anything. Even cupboards *bhi nahi the, clothes rakhne ke liye. Ek hi gadda tha. Saat din tak* I didn't have gas cylinder, stove. *Aisa, matlab kuch bhi nahi tha, actually, ghar mein*. But still, I was very very happy."

There were a few issues though. Sunil was constantly hanging out with his friends and paid no attention to his wife. Every night he would ask someone or the other to come over and Swati would have to make dinner for them. Most nights, there was nothing left for her to eat.

"Pyaaz tamatar daal mein murmure milake kitni baar khaya hai."

At the same time, the pressures of earning for a large family were increasing day by day. Sunil's father had passed away and the responsibility of the whole family was now on him. This tension was getting between the couple. *Par kisi tarah gaadi aage badh rahi thi…*

Along with Sunil, Swati was also working, as a primary school teacher. At the end of the month, even though Sunil was running a business of his own, Swati would earn more than him. But instead of appreciating her, Sunil would tell her every day, *"Tu bewakoof hai, tujh mein akal nahin hai!"* But the young wife swallowed her pride, never complained.

As their kids grew up, the time Swati could spend with her husband became limited. They spoke seldom, and only about household matters. *Saath rehte toh the magar unki duniya bilkul alag thi.*

Till one morning, while her husband was in the bathroom, Swati heard a 'ping' on his phone. She casually picked it up and read an SMS. It said, 'Please don't leave me.' What a strange message! Her gut said – something is not right.

Despite her husband's reassurance, Swati called up the number. A woman answered and told her that she had borrowed some money from Sunil, which she was not able to return. So she was scared that Sunil would stop being her friend.

Swati confronted Sunil, who immediately backed up the woman's story.

"Maine bola, okay fine. Abhi toh paise aagaye, nahi bhi aayenge toh forget that money. Abhi chhor do usko. He convinced me *ki, haan theek hai – main nahi baat karunga, main nahi milunga. Maine bola, okay."* Swati had strong faith in her husband.

"I trusted him again. *Bewakoof nahi hoon, par buddhu toh hoon hi."*

That December, Sunil insisted that Swati and the kids visit her parents' home in Nagpur. Swati found this odd because she had gone to her *maika* just the previous month.

Even their phone calls during this holiday were short, and Swati found out from her mother-in-law that Sunil stayed away from home all night.

Throughout her holiday, Swati was tormented by doubt. And no matter how much she tried to ignore it, her mind was uneasy. So she decided to confront him when she returned home.

When he dismissed her questions, she hugged him tight, hoping against hope that she was wrong.

"Jab usne accept kar liya, toh I didnt say anything. *Main kuch bol hi nahin paayi* for two days. I just sat on the sofa, hall *mein. Do din ke baad phir* I talked to him. *Phir maine chillaana shuru kiya aur phir main dheere dheere bahut aggressive hone lagi."*

Swati's only support systems through all of this were her two childhood friends, who were living in the US. Even after a long day at work, they would stay up all night to talk to her. Reassure her, give her strength.

Finally, Swati decided to tell her mother-in-law about Sunil's affair. Seeing that his family was against him, Sunil apologised and told everyone *ki main sab sahi kar doonga.*

Par bolne aur karne mein bahut farak hota hai. And soon, Sunil went back to his old ways. He knew that Swati loved him too much to leave him. Due to this confidence, Sunil started ignoring her completely. When Swati wanted to talk about something, he would shout at her.

Swati's in-laws could see what was happening, so when she left home for the first time, they called her every day and said – *beti, waapas aa ja*. She relented when Sunil agreed to follow a set of rules that Swati's aunt (a judge) had drafted.

I have always wanted ki main apni zindagi apne hisab se jiyoon. Lekin apna womamhood kabhi cherish nahi kar payi. Bhaley hi ab main akeli hoon, magar khud ke liye respect ab aaya hai.

This never happened. But Swati kept quiet because she wanted her kids to have a normal childhood in a normal home. She tried different things like *vaastu shastra* and astrology to solve her problems, but nothing worked.

In fact, things only got worse.

Slowly, Sunil started turning his mother and brother against Swati. And his own behaviour worsened.

Every day Sunil would get irritated with Swati. Every night, he would shout at her. Things were getting so bad that Swati was now afraid of him.

"Woh self lock se chabi khol ke andar aata tha. Chaabi ki awaz mujhe bahut disturb karti thi… Main takiya wakiya sab aise kaan pe rakh ke soti thi ki mujhe woh pata na chale ki woh ghar kitne baje aya hai woh."

This went on until, one day, she got a phone call. It was from the husband of the lady whom Sunil was having an affair with. He gave her the address of a flat and said that this was where Sunil met his wife. Then he added, "If you don't believe me, go now and check."

Swati called up her parents and the aunt who was a judge, and went with them to the flat. There she saw Sunil climbing down a flight of stairs with the other woman. Swati had been calm till then because, for her, the affair was still an abstract idea. Now, it suddenly became too real. She couldn't stop staring at the other woman.

"Meri life mein, utne years mein kabhi bhi himmat nahin hui thi... Maine actually jaake slap kiya dono ko. Pehle husband ko kiya aur baad mein lady ko kiya. Maine koi jawab nahin diya aur hum log wapis aagaye."

Now, Swati saw no reason to stay with her in-laws. She was simply an unpaid servant and doormat in their house. So she left for Nagpur. The kids stayed with her mother-in-law because Swati did not want to disrupt their school schedule.

In between, she returned once when her mother-in-law requested her to take care of the children while she was travelling to Malaysia. Swati hoped that Sunil would not trouble her while she was in Pune at his home. In fact, she hoped he wouldn't come home at all so that they could avoid fights.

But one day he turned up. *"Mujhe chaanta maar ke gaya. Tune mujhe ek baar mara tha na, abhi ek ka toh badla le liya doosra usko bhi mara naa, uska bhi badla loonga. Aisa kehke phir chala gaya."*

Swati was shocked. For several hours she sat trying to process what had happened, almost numb to the pain. Finally she vowed to leave that house forever.

And once the school term ended, she took her children with her to Nagpur, never to return.

"Mere paas kuch nahi tha." With the help of her own family and some generous friends, Swati started to build a new life for herself. She found a small house on rent near her parents' home. And she got busy in taking care of her kids and making it a home.

By now her children had understood that something really bad was happening. *"Parth bas rota rehta tha. Simran thodi sehmi si thi."*

Her immediate concern was taking care of her children. She had filed a domestic violence case against

Sunil and was fighting for her rights and her alimony.

At the time, her friend, who was an astrologer, convinced her to start a small gemstones business. By now, Swati had become interested in spirituality and past-life regression therapy, so what could be better than starting a business related to it?

Before that she had also applied for a job and had immediately got one. That had made her more self-confident. "I was very happy that *ki chalo abb meri life mein thoda ek confidence aaya ki main sach mein bewakoof nahin hoon."*

All this time, Swati was concerned about Simran, her teenage daughter. "I have wholeheartedly tried *ki kahin uska woh innocence nahin jaaye kyunki woh itna kuch dekhte hain abhi. Simran kisiko easily trust karegi hi nahin. Mera basic nature trusting hai.* I still keep on telling her *ki log trustworthy hote hain. Ek person ne agar cheat kiya hai toh* it doesn't mean *ki saare log ek jaise hain. Bas* you have to be careful."

It was easier with Parth. He was still very young when all this happened. *"Ab woh khelta hai. Ab toh woh yaad bhi nahin karta. Maine kabhi nahin suna bachchon se ek baar bhi ki humko Papa se milna hai."*

This was her whole family now – *thoda Band-Aid laga hua family, but family.*

Today's Swati is nothing like the old Swati who had let people take her for granted. She is sweet, witty and confident. She has her own apartment and takes care of her children. The gemstones business is doing well, and she has even started a small saree designing business called Parsim. The best part is that her children are very proud of her. For Simran, her mother is her hero. For Parth, she is someone he can share everything with.

"13-year-old boys don't talk about weaknesses with their mother. But Parth sensitive *hai. Woh baat karta hai. Woh brave bhi hai. Isiliye baat karta hai woh sab ke baare mein."*

A woman must never give up her self-respect. Not even for her husband.

After years of emotional and verbal abuse from Sunil, Swati can look into the mirror and say to herself, *"Tu bewakoof nahi hai."*

You are bold, beautiful, wonderful, unique. *Naari kamzor nahin, woh hai shakti ka roop. Apna wo sundar roop nikhaaro, apna jeevan sudhaaro.*

Be that amazing woman you were meant to be.

Being Human

Jyoti Dhawale
Mumbai, Maharashtra

"HIV positive hai – don't touch." People think HIV is a death sentence. But Jyoti Dhawale and her husband Vivek Surve are leading a normal married life. Proving that love is the most powerful force in the world. More powerful than fear.

Jyoti Dhawale was the daughter of an air force officer. She spent her childhood in the safety of military cantonments around the world. But inside her home, it was a different matter. Jyoti had a cruel mother, who kept her locked up in a small room and ill-treated her.

"Subah ka nashte mein cornflakes aur doodh milta tha. Jiske andar chote chote keede milte the." And at night they used to always give *"dudh-bread, dudh-bread, dudh-bread all the time"*. Lunch was the only proper meal she had but, of course, there were no second helpings.

Jyoti grew up feeling unloved and alone. And from the time she was three, she has suffered from a hearing disability.

When she finally told her friends in school about the way her mother treated her, they were shocked. One of them asked: *"Kya yeh tumhari sauteli ma toh nahin hai?"*

Jyoti was stunned. She had never questioned who her mother was before. But thinking about it, she did act the way stepmothers did in films.

In 9th standard, Jyoti was made to meet a woman she felt instantly connected to. *"Yeh tumhari real mummy hai,"* her grandparents told her. Jyoti could not process this news. As a result, she failed 9th standard.

Jaise-taise, she finished studying till 12th standard by enrolling at NIOS (National Institute of Open Schooling). But the situation at home was only getting worse. So she decided to run away.

A gutsy but frightened 18-year-old girl, she moved from city to city looking for a job. Pune to Ranchi, Ranchi to Delhi, Delhi to Raipur and then finally to Mumbai. Without a degree, steady salary or a support system – those were tough days for Jyoti. But she carried on, because going back 'home' wasn't an option.

Finally, Jyoti landed up in Mumbai and found a job as a teacher at a school for deaf children in Goregaon. Things were looking up. She had a stable job and some friends in the city. That is when she met her husband.

After years of feeling unwanted, when her husband told her that he fell for her from day one, Jyoti instantly fell in love with him. *Chat mangni, pat shaadi*. And within a few months, she was pregnant.

Jyoti's joy knew no bounds. Finally, she was going to have a family of her own. The early days of her marriage had been wonderful, and she couldn't wait to tell her husband the good news.

But when she finally told him, his response shocked

her. *"Abort kar do. Abhi bachcha nahin sambhal sakte."*

A part of Jyoti wanted to resist, but she felt she had to obey her husband's command. After all, she was financially and emotionally dependent on him.

That was the first time she aborted her baby. In one year, she aborted three more babies. Each time, she railed against her husband.

"Don't you have any feelings for these babies? If you don't want a child, why don't you wear a condom?"

He replied, "I don't like condoms."

So many back-to-back abortions made her body ache. But her protests fell on deaf ears. Each time, she would be forced to abort in a different hospital.

Jyoti tried several ways to avoid pregnancy as well, but nothing worked. She was allergic to oral contraceptives and, with vaginal contraceptives, she had to wait 10-15 minutes before engaging in sex. When she would tell her husband to wait while she prepared herself, he would not listen and pounce on her. At the time, Jyoti had no idea about marital rape and the Domestic Violence Act. And she felt that her submission was taken as consent.

Life continued in this way until Jyoti learnt that she was pregnant for the fourth time. This time, after the routine tests that precede the abortion procedure were completed, the doctor asked to meet them.

Strange. None of the other doctors had asked for such a meeting.

"You are HIV positive," she said. Jyoti couldn't believe her ears. How could this happen? How could she have got this virus?

The doctor continued: "Jyoti, you can continue with this pregnancy even if you are HIV positive. With regular doses of Anti Retroviral Treatment, there is less than 5% chance that your baby will be HIV positive. But if you abort now, this may be your last chance to have a baby." At the time, doctors believed that abstinence was the only option for HIV-positive patients. Since the knowledge of PReP, an oral medicine that lowers the risk of contracting HIV by 90%, was not widespread.

The doctor's words rang clear as a bell in Jyoti's head. And all she could think about was the little baby inside her.

"I want to go ahead with my pregnancy," she blurted. And that was that. In front of the doctor, Jyoti's husband had no choice but to agree.

Back home, Jyoti began a rigorous schedule of Anti Retroviral Treatment. Twice a day, at a fixed time, she had to take her medicines. No delay in taking the dose could be tolerated.

But the shock of being HIV positive had still not worn off. *Aisa kyun hua mere saath? Why me?* All Jyoti knew was that HIV was a sexually-transmitted disease. But neither she nor her husband had multiple partners. In fact, her husband had tested HIV negative.

Then she remembered all the tests she had undergone during her three abortions. What if one of the hospitals had transfused her with infected blood? But each time she had got an abortion she had destroyed the papers, so there was no way to tell which hospital was responsible.

Till this day, Jyoti believes that's how she was infected.

Six months after she got this horrific news, Jyoti gave birth to a beautiful, HIV-negative, baby boy. They named him Lalitesh.

During this time, Jyoti started noticing that her husband had changed. He had become distant and often talked secretively on the phone. He had also started refusing to pay for medical treatment. Without it, Jyoti's life was in serious danger.

So she decided to take matters into her own hands. She found a job on the Internet at an IT company in

Bangalore. And, in desperation, she left her baby and husband to work in Bangalore.

Within a month, she got a call from her maid. *"Aap wapas aa jao. Ghar mein kuch theek nahin hai."*

When she got home, Jyoti found out. Her husband was having an affair. And he wanted a divorce. Jyoti felt like her world was coming apart at the seams. She begged and pleaded with her husband. She even spoke to the lady he was having an affair with. But nothing worked.

Every day her husband would fight with her, trying desperately to wear her down. But Jyoti wanted to save her marriage at any cost.

But when the fights became violent, Jyoti's friends advised her to grant the divorce. And when she felt like she had no choice, Jyoti finally signed the papers.

Dark days followed for Jyoti. Depressed and lonely, she missed her baby the most. Her husband had got legal custody of their son, and Jyoti was not allowed to meet him. Even her father's family did not reach out to her because they had branded her 'characterless'. For running away from home.

But in these darkest hours, hope came from other unlikely places.

Jyoti was working night shifts in a software company, but was finding it increasingly difficult to manage her health and her work hours. So, she approached her team leader to ask for better work hours.

"Why? I can't change your timings just like that. You better have a good reason."

"I have a condition – I am HIV positive. These hours cause problems for my health."

The team leader was shocked, but gathering his wits, he promised her that he would discuss this with his bosses discreetly and help her out.

Soon, Jyoti was told to appear for a meeting with the head of HR and a few senior people to discuss her HIV status. Jyoti prepared herself for the worst – they would fire her from the job because of HIV. But after asking her a volley of questions, they said, "Okay. Your work is good and, because of your condition, we'll change your timings."

That act of faith and compassion gave Jyoti hope. If they had supported her, maybe others would too.

Extraordinarily that came true for her.

Jyoti met a man called Vivek Surve in an online chat room. She had rejected his friend requests many times

What is the difference between HIV and AIDS? Can I get it by touching or kissing? (The answer is 'no'.)

before, but he was persistent. Finally, she accepted it. They chatted for six months, but somehow the conversation never progressed beyond the usual pleasantries.

But when Jyoti's father passed away, and her stepmother refused to let her near him, Vivek was the unexpected friend she leaned on.

"Anger and hatred for my stepmother, and grief over my father's death was eating me up. My best friend was in Dubai but Vivek, my new friend, drove all the way to be with me, emotionally and physically."

Jyoti was deeply touched by his kindness, and the two decided to meet up the following weekend.

Soon after, the friendship turned into something more and the two began dating. Jyoti had not told him about her HIV status. She told herself she would tell him when she was ready.

Finally, when things were getting serious, she

confided in him.

Vivek's response was as expected.

"You're telling me all this after three months!" Vivek thought of all the times he had kissed her. Now he was scared: "What if I get HIV?"

Vivek disappeared from Jyoti's life for three months. No calls, no messages. Nothing. Jyoti told herself, *"Chalo koi baat nahin. Jo hua accha hua* – maybe he was not meant for me." And decided to move on.

But somewhere deep inside her heart, she still longed for Vivek. And Vivek, despite what he told himself, also missed her.

For three months, Vivek went from one doctor to another to get more information on HIV. What is the difference between HIV and AIDS? Can I get it by touching or kissing? Should I stay away from Jyoti?

Eventually, Vivek SMSed Jyoti – 'I want to meet you. Can I come to your house?' When they met, he explained to her that he was scared, but his love had not diminished.

"What if you leave again? How can I trust you?"

"I am scared, but stay with me while I work through this."

Jyoti decided to stay.

Two years later, Jyoti married Vivek. Initially Vivek's parents were opposed to the match, but after seeing their commitment to each other, they relented.

Even after marriage, Jyoti knew that her in-laws were scared – not of her, but of her disease. But gradually, Vivek and Jyoti were able to prove to them that HIV cannot be passed on by saliva or by touch. That a HIV positive person can be loved like anyone else.

Today, Jyoti is an HIV activist, an ambassador of Beydaar (a Pakistani NGO), an advisor for The Well Project (a non-profit dedicated to creating awareness among women about HIV and AIDS) and a blogger for The Girl Like Me, a program by The Well Project.

Even her mother-in-law, who had once told her, *"ki publicity mein mat aao"*, is today very proud of her.

And Vivek and Jyoti's love story is a *misaal* for all those people who think HIV-positive people cannot lead normal lives with HIV-negative partners.

Because love is a virus that can't be defeated. Not by society – not by stigma. It only grows and fills the heart with hope. For a wonderful new future.

Bindaas

Bindaas ladki ka matlab wo jo thodi 'cool' ho. Lekin bindaas hone ki asli nishani kapdon se ya accent se nahi, apni soch se pata chalti hai.*

*A bindaas girl is one who is considered 'cool'. But bindaas isn't about wearing cool clothes or speaking with an accent, it's a state of mind, an attitude.

You Can Do Magic

Sanam Karunakar
Mumbai, Maharasthra

"Zindagi ek safar hai suhana – yahan kal kya ho, kisne jaana." Life can change in an instant – for better or for worse. Sanam's life took a terrifying turn when she was 16. But instead of crying, cursing and feeling low, Sanam bounced back. And found a new zest for life.

At 5 o'clock in the morning on 17 April 1995, Sanam and her family met with an accident. The car in which they were travelling was hit by an ST bus right outside Sancheti Hospital in Pune. For six long days, Sanam battled for her life, slipping in and out of consciousness. When she finally woke up, the 16-year-old had a nine-kg traction on her neck.

"I could not move any part of my body below the chest. I could not even *feel* anything."

Sanam had suffered a severe spinal cord injury. She was paralysed from the chest down.

But worse was yet to come. On the 10th day after the accident, Sanam learnt that her parents were no more.

"I cried for days ... I could not accept what had happened."

Perhaps this is a bad dream, I will wake up and find everything is 'normal'.

Sadly, it was all too real. The only miracle was that Ayesha, Sanam's younger sister who had fallen out of the car on impact, had received just a few minor injuries.

It was *naani* who took charge of the situation at this difficult time and decided to shift her to Mumbai. Sanam spent the next 11 months in the Parsi General

Hospital with *naani* at her bedside night and day. As she underwent one surgery after another.

Why me? Why did God leave me behind to suffer?

Sanam could not control her urine or bowels. And lying in one position all day, she got a very bad bed sore.

"It took an hour-and-a-half each day to clean, scrub and change the dressing."

Ultimately, Sanam underwent corrective plastic surgery, followed by a complicated procedure called 'tendon transfer'. Here, muscles from Sanam's leg were transferred to her fingers, to improve their grip.

"The stitches were tiny and dug into my skin.... I remember it was the most painful of all my operations."

What will I do with these fingers? What is my future?

Finally, the doctor said Sanam was well enough to go home. She was shifted to *naani's* house — with two nurses to take care of her around-the-clock. This was expensive but necessary. Thankfully, Sanam was born a Parsi, so financial help came from various community trusts.

"There was a lady called Scylla Vatcha who was an angel for us."

A year or two passed, things settled into a routine. But Sanam continued to feel sad and hopeless. At this point, *naani* heard about a hospital called the Indian Spinal Injury Centre in New Delhi. Sanam was admitted there for three months. It was a major turning point in her life.

"Mostly, patients were depressed, but there was one guy who used to be an athlete who had such a positive spirit!"

It was here that Sanam learnt many small but important skills, like tying shoelaces, opening zips, holding a pen, eating with a spoon. The 'impossible' suddenly became possible.

Show me, tell me, teach me more. I want to live, I want to grow!

Sanam was taught how to sleep on a normal bed instead of a hospital bed. How to shift from bed to chair. And even how to sit in a car.

"I went to see the sights of Delhi – I enjoyed it and felt so much better."

When Sanam returned to Mumbai, she was happier and more confident. *Naani* decided it was time for some changes. She wanted to make the girls independent, so she shifted out. Sanam and Ayesha were now on their own.

"I started managing the house, took up some data

entry work and joined a college. They exempted me from lectures but I went for the exams."

Luckily Sanam had a loyal bunch of friends to hang out with at home. Like other teenagers, they chit-chatted, studied and even did harmless *masti* together. One of their favourite pastimes was making prank calls.

One day, Sanam's friend Vineeta dropped by. She said, "You know there's a really cute guy who lives in the building opposite mine. Let's prank call him."

Sanam readily agreed. From somewhere, they got his number and called him.

"Hi, my name is Pia," Sanam lied.

That was the day Sanam 'met' Suraj. They hit it off and started chatting regularly – swapping stories about their lives, college and family. Often, Sanam made up stories about college since she studied from home. But the conversations made her happy, they made her feel normal.

One day, Suraj asked for her email id. He wanted to chat with her on MSN Messenger. Sanam now had a confession to make.

"My name is not Pia … it is Sanam. I changed it because my first call to you was a prank."

"Cool," he replied. And that was the end of that.

For hours on end, Sanam and Suraj chatted on MSN. They even played two-player games, like pool, online. Sanam waited patiently all day for Suraj to return from work so they could continue their conversations.

Finally, one fine day, Suraj proposed that they meet. Now, Sanam got really scared. She hadn't told him her big secret. She wasn't just any other girl, she was a girl in a wheelchair. Would Suraj remain her friend once he discovered the truth?

Sanam's friend reassured her, "He is a nice guy, from a good family. We know where he lives. Just be honest. Everything will be okay."

Gathering courage, Sanam told Suraj everything. At first he did not believe her. Was it yet another prank on her part, or was she making up excuses because she didn't want to meet him? Suraj was furious.

"If you don't want to meet me, just say so. Don't make up stories!" he yelled.

"I swear, I am speaking the truth," replied Sanam

"Then give me your address, I want to come meet you right now," said Suraj. Sanam gave her address, but he never showed up.

But they continued to talk on the phone and things

went back to normal.

Till one evening when Sanam and her friends were chilling at home, the doorbell rang and in walked a boy she had never seen before.

"Who are you?" Sanam asked.

"Guess *karo*," he replied.

But Sanam was clueless.

"Who are you?" she asked again.

"Suraj," he said with a broad smile.

"*Kaun* Suraj?" she thought to herself. And then it suddenly hit her. "Oh my God! It's you!"

The shock quickly turned into excitement and then happiness as the two friends could not stop talking. It was perfect. No awkwardness of meeting for the first time. The conversation just flowed.

In the few hours that Suraj and Sanam spoke that evening, she shared everything with him. About her accident, her surgeries, all the pain and helplessness. And how she was slowly but surely becoming better. When he finally left, it was with the promise of meeting more often.

With Suraj, Sanam started venturing out of her home for 'dates' at restaurants around the city. At first it was difficult. How would he carry her from the wheelchair to the taxi? But Suraj simply said, "You show me how to do it, and we will do it." And he did, with the help of a kindhearted taxi driver called Raju.

Very easily and very naturally, Sanam fell in love with Suraj. When she told her friends about these feelings, they advised her to keep quiet, saying, If he feels the same way, let him tell you. Otherwise you will lose your friendship.

How can I expect a normal boy to fall in love with me? It's best I stay silent.

Until one day, out of the blue, Suraj blurted out, "Will you marry me?" Sanam's heart stopped.

She asked hesitatingly, "Are you sure you want to be with me in spite of my problems?"

"I love you and I can take care of you," he said sweetly and confidently.

"Then I will marry you," she replied, bursting with joy.

But Sanam was only 23, Suraj 24. Their families were not convinced. A hundred questions were asked on both sides. What if Suraj changed his mind in the future, what if he could not cope? What about money

"If I am here, God has a purpose for me.
I have to keep living, keep dreaming....
How can I stop?"

and stability – how would they manage, where would they live?

"His parents were against it, my sister was against it."

As long as we have each other, we will find a way.

On 23 September 2003, accompanied only by a few friends, Suraj and Sanam had a court marriage. For two years, neither family knew about their wedding. But a secret this big cannot be kept forever.

Suraj's mother found the marriage certificate and all hell broke loose. There was some screaming and shouting, and a whole lot of drama. But eventually the families relented and decided to hold a reception for the couple.

Suraj moved into Sanam's flat and they began a new life together.

Sanam and Suraj's love story is the stuff of fairytales. And the element of magic was brought in by a cute, furry Labrador – Magic.

The year was 2002. Sanam's story was featured in *Bombay Times*. Soon after, she received a call from Shirin Merchant, representing 'Canines Can Care'. Shirin had just introduced the concept of 'assistance dogs' in India.

"Would you like a dog that is trained to help you with everyday tasks?" asked Shirin.

Sanam liked the idea. And that's how a five-month-old black Labrador puppy called Magic became a part of her life. *Badi badi aankhen, chhoti chhoti harkatein...* Magic brought a whole lot of love and positive energy into Sanam's life.

In fact, before her accident, Sanam had always dreamed of being a vet. Having a pet was the next best thing.

There was just one problem. Magic was a hyperactive dog — could he really be trained?

"Yes," said Shirin. "We will train him to do simple tasks like picking up dropped objects, switching on the light."

And, sure enough, Magic soon learnt these things. Suraj and Sanam were girlfriend-boyfriend back then. And they spent many evenings training Magic. They even accompanied Shirin for a weeklong dog-training course.

"We used to practice what we learnt with Magic. It was amazing how fast he used to pick up things!"

Suraj and Sanam started taking Magic for demonstrations at the Kennel Club of India's dog shows. And to various schools so that they could create awareness about assistance dogs.

One day Sanam said to Shirin, "I am doing this boring data entry work. I wish there was something else to keep me busy!"

Shirin proposed a novel idea. "You have a way with animals. Why not start a boarding house for dogs?"

Will I be able to handle this? Okay, let me try.

The first doggie client was a basset hound whose owner was leaving for a vacation. Through Shirin's reference, many more pets started coming in. Clients were happy because, with Sanam, their beloved pets were loved and cared for.

"Yes, I had help to walk the dogs thrice a day. Everything else I could manage."

That's how, sitting in a wheelchair, Sanam started a whole new business called 'Perfect Pooch'. She started with two–three dogs at a time – that was 13 years ago.

Now, they manage 10–12 dogs at a time.

Suraj has quit his job to join the business (it now makes good money!).

"There is so much demand, especially at Diwali and Christmas, that we have to turn people down."

A perfect husband, an adorable pet and loving in-laws – the only missing piece was a baby. Can I be a mom too?

Six years ago, Sanam and Suraj shifted from Grant Road to a more spacious house in Powai. And they felt it was time to start a family. At first they tried to adopt, but were rejected as 'unfit parents'.

That's when they thought of IVF (in-vitro fertilisation) as an option. It was an expensive affair, but perhaps God heard their prayers.

Because 16 years after the accident that shattered her life, Sanam won the case filed against the bus company. She received a sizable cash settlement.

"We decided to use the money to conceive a child through IVF."

Doctors agreed that Sanam's ovaries were healthy. Her eggs could be fertilised. But she would not be able to carry the child.

With the help of an organisation called Surrogacy

India, Sanam and Suraj got a very good set of doctors. And they found a surrogate — the woman whose womb would be home to their child for nine months.

The couple now had to undergo IVF, wherein the egg and sperm from the parents would be 'mated' in a petri dish. This is a tricky process, and it usually never works in the first go.

"We were lucky – in our first attempt there were three viable embryos. One little monster survived!"

Holding the newborn in their arms was a magical moment for both mumma and papa. Now three years old, Rayaan has turned his parents' world upside-down. He is a joy, he is a terror.

"Managing 10 dogs is easier than managing one toddler!"

Today, Sanam's dream is to have a beautiful big house with a garden where babies and doggies can run around together.

That would mean shifting to the outskirts of Mumbai, to a farmhouse. And God willing, it will happen very soon.

Sanam could have given up, she could have given in. But somehow she found the strength to be positive.

Pizza Granny

Padma Srinivasan
Bengaluru, Karnataka

"You are retired – your life is over." But Padma Srinivasan found a new goal and new purpose after 60. And it gave her life new meaning. She walks each day with a spring in her step and a twinkle in her eye.

Padma Srinivasan was born into a well-to-do Tamil Brahmin family in Madurai.

"My family was very protective, very conservative. I was sent to a convent school, followed by a women's college."

Padma completed her B.A. in zoology and botany, her only option as a 'science' student. At the age of 18, she got married to her maternal cousin and shifted to Bangalore. Soon after, she gave birth to her daughter, followed by her son.

"I was a happy housewife … busy in the kitchen and the four walls of my home."

All this changed when her husband Srinivasan met with a fatal accident. Padma's entire world came crashing down. She was not even 30 years old.

"I was completely devastated. My daughter was 11 and my son just a toddler…"

Slowly, it sunk in – the responsibility of raising these two children was on her frail shoulders. She was not even used to going to the market alone … how would she manage?

"You are still young. I will look for a boy and get you married again," said her father-in-law. But Padma refused. She had only one goal in mind — to give her children a good upbringing. To do that, she would have to step out of her cocoon.

"No woman in my family had ever worked ... I was the first one to do it."

Padma's husband was an engineer with the public sector unit Indian Telephone Industries (ITI) – the company offered her a job on compassionate grounds.

"I accepted the offer and started working as a clerk in their accounts department."

Each day Padma woke up at 4 am to cook, pack lunch, get the kids ready for school. She caught a company bus to the ITI factory at 7 am. After a full day's work she returned at 7 pm, cooked dinner and helped the children with their homework.

"But it was very difficult and stressful.... I often came home and cried."

Her elder sister was a great source of moral support while her parents went a step further. They shifted to Bangalore, so they could look after the children while Padma was at work. And, slowly, Padma found her feet.

"I realised that the working world is tough and I have to be tough to handle it."

Padma became more confident and more ambitious. She realised one thing clearly.

Hard work is not enough. To come up in life, I must study further.

She decided that cost accounting was the best option, as it was a correspondence course. Now Padma's long days got even longer. She would stay up past midnight, surrounded by books, taking down notes, making calculations. For the ICWA exam was not an easy nut to crack.

"There was one paper each in higher mathematics, accountancy, engineering and economics. All the subjects were new for me!"

Padma's father had a friend who was the Head of Department at St John's Military School in Bangalore. This kind gentleman agreed to come home and teach her higher mathematics. The only 'tuition fee' he demanded was a hot cup of coffee.

"Like that, many people helped when I was struggling, when I felt small and alone."

Padma's patient and dedicated efforts bore fruit. It took five years, but she passed all the exams and became a certified cost accountant. Everyone was surprised —

there was new respect for her in their eyes.

The ITI management immediately promoted Padma to the post of Officer — the first female officer in the history of the company. The normal hierarchy was from clerk to senior clerk to accountant to senior accountant and *then* you became an officer.

The management conducted a felicitation meeting where her boss declared, "See, this lady – with all her responsibilities – she has passed the exam. You boys should all learn something from her!"

Padma's *brahmastra* was discipline. She led a disciplined life and expected the same from her children. They used to call her Hitler because she was 'always so strict'.

But it was this tough love that moulded them into responsible young adults.

"My children studied well and never gave me problems – what more could I ask for?"

At the office, Padma continued to rise professionally, but she remained humble and grounded. As the Finance Manager, she was in charge of the provident fund and gratuity section. Due to this, she often met the wives of deceased ITI workers.

When many of these widows came for the final settlement, they were shocked to learn that their husbands had already taken loans, and hence there was hardly any money to disburse.

"I remember this lady who was illiterate and had six children.... She cried in front of me and said, 'Who will take care of us now?'."

Padma was deeply moved by her plight. She tossed and turned in her bed, unable to sleep all night.

"At least I had an education, I had parents to support me ... she has nothing!"

Padma brought up the issue at the staff welfare meeting, but the management shrugged and said, "She is illiterate ... what job can we give?"

It was then that Padma proposed a novel idea. "Let us start a bakery!"

The ITI canteen used to buy Modern bread, Britannia biscuits and cakes from the market. Instead, such items could be made in-house. By whom? Women like that young widow with no hope or support.

"The Chairman immediately agreed and said, 'We will provide the land and the building. But equipment you will have to arrange for'."

Jahaan chaah hai, wahan rah hai.... Padma went from cubicle to cubicle to collect funds. She floated shares and convinced every ITI officer to 'invest' at least ₹1,000. In this manner, she raised ₹4 lakh over a period of one year. The all-women Shree Shakthi bakery was inaugurated in 1983 (and it remains in business till this day).

"This gave me lot of satisfaction ... that in my own small way I could help others."

When Padma Srinivasan retired from her job at the age of 58, this thought remained with her. She had fulfilled her duties and responsibilities. And yet, she did not yearn to sit back and 'enjoy life'.

God sent so many people to help me when I was a zero. I should do something for others now.

Education had played an important role in her life. Perhaps she could start a school?

"No," said her daughter, Sarasa. Schools were mushrooming all across Bangalore. It was more about making money than spreading knowledge.

"You want to help people. Why don't you do something that others aren't doing at all?" said Sarasa.

In fact, from her college days, Padma's daughter

had been inclined towards the plight of the elderly. She remembered her own childhood where her *paati* and *tatta* (grandparents) had placed such an important role.

"Elders need children and children need elders! So we came up with the concept of Vishranthi – an old age home and a children's home in the same premises."

But where would the funding for this ambitious project come from? Padma had purchased a 1-acre plot on the outskirts of Bangalore soon after retirement. But she didn't have the money to construct a building.

"My daughter gave me the idea to prepare and sell pizzas to raise money for it."

Padma approached Amul to take up their franchise. Sarasa taught her mother Padma and mother-in-law Jayashree how to make pizza sauce and toppings. The ladies were now in business – selling tasty cheesy pizzas for ₹5 a slice.

"Although our pizzeria was in the house garage, we got good number of clients!"

On Sundays, Padma and Jayashree took rest while Sarasa manned the counter. On one such day, a little boy came in to eat. After gobbling down the slice he asked, "Where are my grannies – the pizza is not the same!"

While the 'pizza grannies' had become quite famous, their business was not making much profit. *We need ₹1 crore and all I have in my pocket is ₹5 lakh.*

Meanwhile, there was another problem. The land Padma had purchased was agricultural and would have to be converted. The local tehsildar was asking for a ₹3 lakh bribe, which she firmly refused to give. In fact, Padma lost her temper.

"You are asking me – a widow – to pay bribe? Are you not ashamed of yourself?"

The tehsildar was apologetic, "Don't get angry madam – the money is not just for me. It goes to everyone from the peon to the minister."

"To do good, there are always a thousand obstacles."

Magar vighna hai toh vighnaharta bhi hai. In Padma's own life there had been so many obstacles, so many struggles.

As she was struggling with this issue, one fine day Padma picked up the newspaper and her eyes fell on a photograph. It was Mr Krishnappa – who used to be a machine operator in ITI and also a member of the workers' union. He was now an MLA.

"Krishnappa helped me with Shakthi Bakery. Maybe

he can help me now?"

Maybe he does not even remember me.... But she was determined to try.

More than 200 people had gathered for the weekly Janata Darshan. Padma sat in the very last row. Krishnappa entered from the back door and the very first person he set eyes on was Padma.

"Madam!" he cried out. "What are you doing here?"

The MLA was eager to help and even accompanied her to the tehsildar's office.

He said, "Don't you know who this Madam is? Get her work done!"

A week later the conversion order was sent directly to Padma's house. She did not have to pay a single paisa.

At the same time, the pizza business got a boost. Sarasa had a friend in Satyam Computers. She asked him, "Can we sell our pizzas in your staff canteen?" He readily agreed.

On the first day, Padma was nervous. Would the young IT employees like her home-style, vegetarian pizzas? Or would they prefer Dominos?

"I was surprised to find a long queue.... They all wanted *Granny's Pizza*!"

"We give water to the coconut tree at the roots and it gives water back from its head.... So I say you must keep on giving. You will earn the blessings."

Soon, *Granny's Pizza* became a weekly attraction in various companies of Bangalore. Accenture, IBM, Fidelity, Sun Microsystems, HP, Flipkart and Dell.

"I also always wanted the youngsters to know the motive behind our business. I wanted them to know about Vishranthi."

So deep was her commitment that Padma decided to sell her home on Richmond Road. She gave her children their share and used the rest of the money towards building construction. Thus, in 2010, her dream of a homely, clean and green living space for the elderly and for abandoned children finally came into being.

"I did not forget Mr Krishnappa's help ... we invited him to inaugurate the building."

Today, Vishranthi is home to 20 elders and 25 children. When you enter the complex, you feel a sense of peace and of belonging. Senior citizens telling stories to junior citizens. Doing pranayama in the meditation hall or taking a walk near the pond.

"Even pizza toppings come from Vishranthi's vegetable garden!" exclaims Padma with pride.

The grannies have now trained an army of youngsters to make their famous pizzas. But Padma still keeps a close watch on the sauces and freshness of ingredients.

At 80, Padma is still very active and keeps all the accounts. She takes daily rounds of the compound. Supervises the construction work of new dormitories. Watches over the cooks and gardeners.

"But now my health does not permit.... So it is not me, it is Sarasa who is the Managing Trustee."

In 2008, when Padma had an attack of bronchitis, Saras took a decision to quit her job as General Manager at Thai Airways. And help her mother run Vishranthi more systematically.

"We charge a monthly fee of ₹10,000 from senior citizens. But our actual cost is much more."

Profits from the pizza business and fund-raising shows help bridge this gap. The rest comes from well-wishers. How these donations happen, Padma has no idea. *Each day is a small miracle.*

"Some time ago we hardly had ₹3,000 in the bank..." recalls Padma. "I was thinking, how will we pay the staff?"

An NRI walked in the very next day and donated ₹3 lakh in memory of his father.

Bas aapka ek lakshya ho, ek purpose ho toh bhagwan koi raaste nikal deta hai.

Aagey bahut kuch karna hai. Aakhri saas tak, manzil ke paas tak.

Lagey Raho

Apeksha Shah
Mumbai, Maharashtra

'This is too difficult – I can't do it!' We struggle, fail and give up on ourselves. Apeksha Shah found courage at her lowest point. She ran towards her goal slowly and steadily, and won the marathon of her life.

"*Size toh dekh, Vivek ki biwi nahin, aunty lag rahi hai!*"

Apeksha Shah heard her cousin's snide remark but ignored it. This was not the time to spoil the mood – the movie was about to start.

"*Madam – yeh aapka seat hai,*" said the usher, twirling his flashlight.

And then came the shock of all shocks.

"I could barely fit in the seat ... it was so uncomfortable!"

Somehow, Apeksha sat through the film. She could not enjoy Ranbir Kapoor's *jawani* or Deepika's *deewani*.

"*How could I let this happen to myself?*"

And that day, something snapped inside her. *Enough is enough. I weigh 130 kgs. This is something I* cannot *accept.*

That day, Apeksha Shah set out to fight a battle. A battle against the bulge.

"I have always been on the healthier side. People used to describe me as '*badi personality*', which meant: good height, *khaate peete ghar ki ladki*."

But in her school and college years, Apeksha was not considered 'fat'.

Born in a well-to-do Gujarati family, Apeksha's world came crashing down when her father passed away. She was in 10th standard at the time.

The family faced financial problems. So Apeksha had to start working.

"I took up a job at the WHRD (World Human Resource Development) at Dadar, and also took tuitions at home."

Neighbours doubted her 'character', because girls from the Vaghad community were not encouraged to go out and work.

"*Kaise paise kamati hai, pata nahi hai?*"

After all she was not even a graduate, how could she be earning so well?

"I realised early that people have a lot of time to talk about others. The best thing is to ignore them – be positive and work hard."

After graduating from SNDT College, Apeksha got married to Vicky Shah. He owned a corporate-gifting firm with his cousin that was doing quite well.

It was an arranged marriage.

On her wedding day, Apeksha Shah weighed 58 kgs and made a pretty picture with her handsome husband. A new life, a new beginning … Apeksha could not be happier!

Vivek and his family were easy-going. There was no pressure to earn and not much household work either.

"I had a lot of free time – all I did was eat, party, and shop all over town!"

Soon the 58-kilo bride was all of 85 kgs. Round, and getting rounder…

"Being a Jain, I also fasted for Paryushan. And this had a yo-yo effect on my body."

Fasting meant up to 16 days on only water. At the end of the fast, Apeksha would be 80 kgs. Over the next fortnight, she would binge on calorie-rich food. Within a week she would gain 10–15 kgs.

"Somehow this just became my way of life…"

Tired of just having fun, Apeksha enrolled for an ECCE (Early Childhood Care and Education) course with Oxford Reading Tree, India. And got a job offer.

Her father-in-law said, "Apeksha – why work for others. Why not for yourself!"

That conversation inspired her to study further. She enrolled for a law course at Lala Lajpat Rai College.

"In the second year of the degree course, I got pregnant."

That's when her weight really went out of hand. Food was her weakness, now it was her craving. Especially the unhealthy kind.

"I was 95 kgs when I conceived. In the ninth month,

my weight was 125 kgs!"

But Apeksha kept thinking – it's okay. *Once I deliver, I will work it off.*

In her third trimester Apeksha also appeared for her 2nd year LLB exams.

It was a normal delivery. A healthy baby girl was born on 28 March 2007.

Apeksha came home with baby Hasti. She weighed 110 kg. Finding it difficult to manage the baby and her studies, Apeksha took a break from college.

"I decided that until Hasti goes to play school, I will focus only on her."

Sitting at home, 10 more kgs piled up. The only silver lining in this fat cloud was that Vicky never once taunted her.

But others did not hesitate to giggle or stare. And it hurt.

"I used to avoid family photo sessions – I felt I was the ugliest in the frame."

Apeksha decided to get busy, to start doing something.

"I had a passion to dress well, so decided to open a boutique."

The shop started doing well but there was one big

disappointment for Apeksha. She designed beautiful outfits for others, but she could not wear any of them herself.

"My tailor would laugh and say, *'Madam, yeh design aapko suit nahi karega'.*"

He was right. And it was heart-breaking.

On impulse, Apeksha took an annual membership at the gym near her home. But after just three days, she gave up.

"Everyone in the gym was hot and I was not. This gave me a huge complex."

This cycle would repeat the next year when there was a newspaper ad screaming, 'Pay this much – lose this much!'

"All I lost was my money … my weight remained a three-digit figure."

Apeksha felt stuck. She felt pathetic. She felt depressed.

She decided to sign up for naturopathy treatment in Bangalore. But then heard about a friend who'd been to the centre and lost 10 kgs in a week. Only to gain it all back in a fortnight.

"I rejected all 'passive slimming' procedures. They simply do not work."

At 130 kg, the only medical solution was 'bariatric surgery'. An operation to reduce the size of one's stomach and hence reduce one's appetite.

Apeksha was convinced 'this is it', and discussed the idea with Dr Srishti, a general physician and family friend.

"I can't say 'yes' or 'no' – you should understand the pros and cons before you decide," said the doctor.

Apeksha visited hospitals, spoke to surgeons. As well as patients who had undergone the procedure. The feedback was mixed – there could be complications. You could eat very little – mostly liquids.

"But I still felt, *'Mujhe karna hai'*. I was simply tired of being fat!"

Apeksha got her file ready and then spoke to her husband. Soon, very soon, life would change for both of them....

"The operation will cost ₹5 lakh... But I promise in two months you will have a slim and sexy wife."

Vicky was calm. He went through the file and finally said, "You are fit. No sugar, no thyroid, no BP. Why the hell are you playing with your body?"

Apeksha was stunned. But there was more to come...

"I love you as you are. But if you want to lose weight, I will support you. Take all the money you need but do it *without* surgery."

It was a turning point for Apeksha.

My God, he believes in me more than I believe in myself!

Thus began the road to recovery. An uncharted path with many an obstacle.

To correct her eating habits, Apeksha consulted a dietician. She was good – but the diet required exotic ingredients like oats, olives and broccoli. It didn't suit Apeksha's desi tastebuds.

But the visit was not in vain.

"I understood that the most important aspect of food is nutrition. I can eat, but I have to eat what is *right* for my body!"

With help from Google, Apeksha created a diet plan for herself. Using common recipes and ingredients found in Gujarati homes.

The second – and more difficult – step was sticking to the diet. Despite the endless social functions in the community.

"I had to make myself strong and avoid unhealthy food. I learnt to say 'no'."

When somebody offered a snack that was not good for her, Apeksha politely said "*Mane nathi bhavtu.*"

"I never said I am dieting because that led to endless comments."

"I felt trapped by my body and responsibilities – most women go through this."

And mostly, it worked. If someone felt really hurt, Apeksha would pretend to eat and hide the food in her purse when no one was looking.

"I refused to make my stomach a dustbin for once!"

The next big step was entering the gym. On the first day, Apeksha could not stay on the treadmill – even at a speed of 4 km per hour.

"My legs didn't fit in the weight-training machines, and my bones made scary sounds."

She went home dejected. That's when Vicky suggested she work out with a reputed trainer, Mahesh Kadam.

His first piece of advice was, "Stop looking at others – focus on your goal!"

In the beginning, the trainer made Apeksha do floor exercises. Although she did not lose any weight in the first month, she felt much lighter.

"I felt motivated to keep going!"

Mahesh devised new workouts, which made the

sessions interesting. And soon, she got results. In just six months, Apeksha lost 15 kgs.

"Nobody else noticed this, but it was a huge boost to my confidence!"

After working out every day for the entire year, Apeksha lost another 25 kgs. In January 2015, she was 98 kilos.

"I was really proud of myself – I had finally done it!"

Continuing with sincerity and commitment, ten months later Apeksha was a sprightly 72 kgs.

At this point, a friend invited Apeksha to participate in an upcoming community marathon called the VRG (Vaghad Runner Group).

"I went to Worli Seaface to see if I could run. But I took 50 minutes to complete 1.5 kms."

Scared of failure, Apeksha refused to participate. But her friend said, "Don't give up so easily. *Try toh kar!*"

Apeksha agreed. There was only a week's time to prepare. For those seven days she trained with Mahesh – just core exercises and running. With correct strides and correct breathing.

The 10-km route began at Worli Seaface, went all the way up Peddar Road, and all the way back. On the uphill stretch, her legs were aching.

But Apeksha did not pause. She did not give in. She did not give up.

"To my surprise, I finished in 66 minutes and stood second! It was a big achievement!"

Apeksha now set her sights on the Standard Chartered Mumbai Marathon. The registration date was close at hand. But to run 21 kms, she would need a 'qualifying certificate'.

"I registered for the 21 kms Virar–Vasai marathon on 21 November 2015."

Her trainer warned, "You are not ready … you will hurt your knees."

But Apeksha was confident. If she could do 10 kms with one week of training, why not 21 kms with three weeks of training?

And she did! Apeksha completed her first 21-km marathon in 2 hours 30 minutes.

"It was tough and I was in pain but I was so happy to reach the finish line!"

That very evening Apeksha told her husband to register her for the 21-km run at SCMM. But the registrations were closed. What to do?

"I didn't want to wait another year… So I ticked 42

kms on the form!"

Vicky was horrified. So was her trainer. Running 42 kms requires at least nine months of training. They had less than two months.

After much convincing, Mahesh Kadam agreed to train Apeksha. Because by now he knew – once she sets her goal, this woman puts in her best. She puts in *everything.*

To motivate herself, Apeksha joined running groups on Facebook and started an FB page to share her progress.

"So many strangers helped me create my running plan. They shared their workouts and diets with me. I couldn't have done it alone!"

Serious runners train before dawn but Apeksha could not join them. She could be on the road only after her daughter left for school.

Despite all these challenges, Apeksha Shah ran the 42-km Standard Chartered Mumbai Marathon on 17 January 2016 and completed it in 5 hours 19 minutes.

As if that was not enough, Apeksha went on to participate in 'Run the Rann', a 42-km desert trail – one of the toughest in Asia. She finished in 11 hours.

Girls from the Vaghad community rarely participate

in sports.

"My in-laws, my mom and many other relatives came to receive me at the station. They were like – *kya se kya ban gayi hai.*"

The girl who would not walk a hundred steps was now running across the country. To the rhythm of her heart. To the beat of her feet.

Many friends and relatives come to Apeksha for advice. She is glad to help.

"People have lost 10–15 kg by following my diet and exercise plan. So far I haven't charged any money."

Apeksha now wants to get certified and make a career in fitness. She plans to focus on young mothers and homemakers, who tend to neglect their health.

"I felt trapped by my body and responsibilities – most women go through this."

But you can be free, you can be happy. It's not rocket science.

"Just set a goal – it could be fitness, or getting back to work, or anything that matters to you. Then work hard to achieve it!"

Feed your soul, not your stomach. You will love what you see in the mirror – a version 2.0 of yourself.

Free to Be Me

Bhavana Issar
Mumbai, Maharashtra

"Ladki on a bike! Odd nahin lagta?" Motorbikes are macho, scootys are girly. It seems like even inanimate objects have a 'sex'. But Bhavana Issar and the bikerni gang prove this theory wrong. Very wrong!

"Aapko bhaari nahi lagta? Kaise chalate ho?"

The security guard at Bhavana's office complex often had such questions. For she was the 'madam who came on a motorbike'.

Back in 1998, in the city of Hyderabad, it was an unusual sight.

A young lady in salwar kameez, on a black Hero Honda Splendour.

"I was in my first job and the bike was perfect for commuting."

By then, Bhavana was used to the stares and even catcalls. In *saadi Dilli*, she rode dad's Bajaj Chetak scooter to college. For she had grown up in a fauji family, where boys and girls were 'equal'.

"I was told – 'Issar women are strong. They can do anything'!"

After graduation, Bhavana went to XLRI Jamshedpur for her MBA. There, she discovered the joy of biking. Many guys on campus had bikes and Bhavana would borrow their keys and hit the road.

"The thrill of riding released some of the pressure I was feeling on campus!"

The boys would sometimes call her 'hunterwali', but

it was mostly in the spirit of fun.

It was when she joined a multinational bank that a colleague made a casual remark which really stung her.

"Oh, so you ride a bike … like those women in *maut ka kunwa*!"

Bhavana felt humiliated but remained quiet. Here was a well-educated, well-travelled man. But it was okay for him to make fun of her passion for bikes. *Because I am a woman.*

Kabhi koi baat sui ki tarah chubh jaati hai. And that's what happened. You want to fit in, you want 'move up in life'.

"By this time I was in Gurgaon, where *everybody* has a car."

So Bhavana gave up the bike for a Maruti 800. Soon after, she connected with her batchmate Gaurav. He too had been a passionate biker in college. But the Yamaha RX 100 was gone, in its place – a Maruti Zen.

The two had been friends for years and decided to get married.

"I was 28 at the time. It was 'late' by conventional standards, but I knew I could not have an arranged marriage!"

The couple moved to Bangalore, where they became sensible workaholics with EMIs to pay off. Three years later, they decided to start a family and adopted a baby girl – Vaanya.

"In Russian that means a 'gracious gift from God'."

At the time, Bhavana was working in Texas Instruments. A hi-tech company with a lot of emphasis on 'people practices'. High on the list was inclusion and gender equality. Yet, Bhavana had to struggle to get maternity leave.

"Mine became the first case where a woman who is adopting was granted the same benefits.... Now it's a done thing."

A woman with a demanding child and a demanding career is often overwhelmed. There is no time for sleep, let alone a hobby.

Bike riding ka toh koi chance hi nahin tha.

And things were fine, life was good. But once in a while, when she met old friends, they would say, "Bhavana – you've changed! Where's that spark!"

Around this time she learnt about Sumedhas, an organisation which conducts workshops on leadership and authenticity. Bhavana signed up for a five-day program and found herself on an inner journey – discovering long-forgotten parts of herself.

"I used to write poetry as a teenager … then it didn't seem 'useful' and I stopped."

At another workshop called 'learning theatre lab', Bhavana talked about her passion for motorcycles. And that triggered a thought – *Start riding again.*

That evening Bhavana came home and said, "Remember how much fun it used to be … let's buy a motorcycle!"

They surveyed the market and both loved the Bullet. Gaurav pulled some strings and managed to get the bike delivered on 11 January 2013 – Bhavana's 39th birthday.

"When I rode out on my Royal Enfield Thunderbird 500cc, I felt that old thrill go up my spine!"

Gaurav was with her on the back seat – with no macho hang-ups.

It was the perfect way for a gal to enter her 40s. Not feeling over the hill but *riding* over the hills.

And it would be even more fun to ride in a group. A Google search led Bhavana to a biker community. But it was an all-men group.

"They wanted to me to 'prove' I was good enough to

join them.… I said – to hell with you!"

That's when Bhavana discovered 'Bikerni' – the largest female biking community in India. And what a difference there was between the two gangs. Unlike the men, Bikernis were warm, generous and open to new members.

On 5 May 2013, Bhavana joined the Bikerni gang for her first long ride. It was also International Women Rider's Day — celebrated on the first Sunday in May each year.

600 bikers set off on their mean machines from Mumbai to Daman. Like-minded women who'd come together, against all odds. Some had fought with their in-laws to pursue this passion. Others had financial struggles.

I won't eat out this month so I can put petrol in my bike.

When you want something, you find a way to make it happen!

In Daman, that evening, the Bikernis slipped into slinky dresses and heels to set the dance floor on fire. Living it up fully, enjoying every moment. Because tomorrow it was back to Mumbai – to deal with a sulking husband.

Bhavana was lucky – she had no such issues.

"Yet, I have chopped and edited myself.... Held myself back....!"

Bhavana continued with her riding and her introspection. But the guilt remained. One Sunday, Bhavana glanced at her husband and daughter – both still sleeping. And she thought, "*Am I allowed to just leave them and go have some fun?*"

Well, it was time to answer that question – loud and clear.

In the summer of 2014, Bikerni Sheetal Bidaye got in touch. She was organising a trip to the highest motorable road in the world, on the Indo–China border.

"Babe, it's going to be amazing. You gotta join us!"

The Mana Pass can be accessed only twice a year: in April and in September. In April 2014, a group of women riders attempted the ride. But they failed to get the necessary permits from the Indo–Tibetan Border force.

The Bikernis decided to try again in September. That's when Bhavana got a chance. But initial euphoria gave way to doubt.

Will I be able to ride in the Himalayas? Am I strong

enough? Ghar kaun sambhalega meri absence mein? How can I leave my family alone for 12 days to go on a 'bike ride'?

To complicate matters, her father-in-law was in hospital with dengue. Her husband was in Delhi, taking care of him. And the household help was on leave. The trip was looking impossible! Maybe next year… But Gaurav would have none of it.

"Don't cancel!" he said. "Dad is recovering… I will be back soon."

There was just one problem. Between Bhavana's departure and Gaurav's arrival there was a gap of two whole days. Who would look after Vaanya?

That's when Bhavana realised it truly takes a village to raise a child. And in the city, where we struggle alone, it's okay to reach out for help. Because friends and neighbours are also 'family'.

"I arranged for my daughter to sleep at her friend's house."

Everything ultimately worked out. Bhavana boarded the train to Dehradun, along with her bike. Leaving her worries behind.

"I had learnt to get off the guilt trip and focus on my road trip!"

"They wanted to me to 'prove' I was good enough to join them.... I said – to hell with you!"

Those 12 days were packed with adventures and experiences.

The Bikernis were welcomed at different locations by NGOs and camera crews. Everywhere, they were asked the same questions.

"Aap ki shaadi ho gayi? Bachche hain? Husband kya karte hain?"

"Husband naukri karte hain aur bachchon ko dekhte hain!" replied the Bikernis.

And the crowds were amazed – *zamana sachmuch badal raha hai.*

On that 1,200-km ride across Uttarakhand, schoolgirls waved at the Bikernis. At Gangotri, a young woman came up to Bhavana and said shyly, *"Aapko dekh kar lagta hai ki hum bhi kar sakte hai."*

That day, Bhavana realised that she was riding for herself, but it was creating an impact on so many others!

A Sikh riding to the holy Hemkund sahib asked Bhavana, *"Tussi Mumbai vich apni Bulletni pe aaye ho?"*

The pilgrim took a selfie with the Bikernis to show his wife.

"Agle saal unko bhi Bulletni pe aana hai aapke saath," said Bhavana.

"Idea acchha hai!" he agreed.

Braving sub-zero weather, rough roads and even wild dogs, the Bikerni gang reached Mana Pass on 5 October 2015. The 'magnificent seven' included Sheetal Bidaye, Kanchan Tamhankar, Trupti Sarmalkar, Shubhangi Manjrekar, Shalaka Zad, Sneh Joshi and, of course, Bikerni Bhavana.

A road trip is not about the destination but the journey itself.

One incident etched in Bhavana's mind is when she lost control of the bike. She lay flat on her back, under the 200-kg Bullet.

"Why am I doing this, is it really worth it?" she thought.

Three Bikernis had gone ahead while three were some distance behind. That's when Bhavana remembered her 'process work'.

When someone is really struggling with an idea, feeling very upset or sorrowful, the trainer says 'stay with it'.

Eventually, you will find a way out.

"I could see an analogy between my inner world and my current reality.… Nobody can help me but myself."

The ride to Mana Pass pushed Bhavana beyond her limits, both physically and mentally. It was also a spiritual experience.

"I no longer have a desire to be 'in control' of everything."

In an earlier era, men ruled the office and women ruled the home. But now marriage is more of a partnership.

"If you want your husband to help with the housework, let him do it *his* way. Or you'll only be stressed."

As for Vaanya – she enjoys long rides and has her very own helmet and kneeguards. The 10-year-old wants to be a fashion designer, adopt stray dogs and ride an Enfield Bullet – just like her mom.

The *aadarsh Indian naari* does not have to wear a big red bindi. She could be the one in a helmet, riding down a different road. Following her own heart.